PRA
BE YOUR OW

'The "god-like genius" of Paul Richards
The title may be opportunistic, but behind the gloss and
the namedropping is a book that provides everything the
spin doctors don't want you to know. Drawing on his own
experiences, the man who as Labour candidate for Billericay
managed to get *Newsnight* to a Labour Party plant sale, helps
you understand how journalists work and teaches that
dealing with the media is a skill not magic – "there are
tricks of the trade and techniques that can be learnt".'
– *Labour Left Briefing*, 1998

'Richards has an acerbic turn of phrase and a good line
in anecdotes. Impressive.'
– *Sunday Telegraph*

'Fabulous'
– *Tribune*

'A useful guide for campaigners and communicators'
– Peter Mandelson

'My only motive for plugging this book is that it is worth reading ... *Be Your Own Spin Doctor* is punchy, clear and well laid out.'
– Phil Woolas

'I am going to urge every colleague and friend in every organisation devoted to returning the centre-left to its democratic socialist traditions to go out, buy a copy, read it and act upon it.'
– Tim Pendry

'A useful guide to good practice in public relations and news management.'
– *Labour Organiser*

'A valuable insight into what needs to be done when dealing professionally with the press.'
– David Hill

HOW TO BE A
SPIN DOCTOR

HOW TO BE A
SPIN DOCTOR

HANDLING THE MEDIA IN THE DIGITAL AGE

Paul Richards

Biteback Publishing

This edition published in Great Britain in 2016 by
Biteback Publishing Ltd
Westminster Tower
3 Albert Embankment
London SE1 7SP
Copyright © Paul Richards 2016
First published in Great Britain 1998 as *Be Your Own Spin Doctor*, by Take That Ltd

ISBN 978-1-84954-998-1

10 9 8 7 6 5 4 3 2 1

A CIP catalogue record for this book is available from the British Library.

Set in Quadraat by Adrian McLaughlin

Printed and bound in Great Britain by
CPI Group (UK) Ltd, Croydon CR0 4YY

MIX
Paper from
responsible sources
FSC® C020471

For Alex and Ollie

The fear of missing out means today's media, more than ever, hunts in a pack. In these modes, it is like a feral beast just tearing people and reputations to bits. But no one dares miss out.

—TONY BLAIR

A politician complaining about the press is like a sailor complaining about the sea.

—ENOCH POWELL

Contents

Introduction

Living in Spin

IT'S NOT THAT long since press officers carried piles of newspapers to the office each morning, when press releases were posted to journalists, when Twitter was what birds did, and mobile phones were the size of loaves of bread.

The digital revolution has changed all that. Today we carry devices in our pockets which can tell us the headline in the *Washington Post*, the weather in Guangzhou, what Putin thinks about Iran, or a picture of a panda sneezing. Today, anyone wanting to influence the media in support of a client, campaign or cause needs to understand how the techniques and tactics have changed, and are changing daily.

The digital revolution is speeding up. There's the famous story of King Louis XVI who wrote in his diary on the very day the Bastille was stormed in 1789: 'nothing'. People living through revolutions usually don't appreciate what's going on around them. That's as true of the revolution in our own times. But just consider how you consume news compared to five years ago, where you get your information from, and how you communicate with other people.

If you're a 'digital native', under the age of around thirty, digital technology is a ubiquitous part of your life, like electricity. You do not consider it at all odd that one of the largest hotel chains, Airbnb, owns no hotels; that the world's biggest taxi company, Uber, owns no taxis; that the world's biggest publisher, Facebook, creates no content. You receive your news and views on a device, from many sources, tailored to your tastes.

The underlying premise of *How to Be a Spin Doctor* is that the spin doctors' trade secrets can be useful to anyone trying to promote a company, client or cause. Those trade secrets are no longer the same. The media landscape, and the ways to navigate and influence it, are so very different from even a decade ago.

Back in the 1990s, the term 'spin doctor' carried more than a little intrigue, excitement and edginess. People wrote novels about them. There was even a band called the Spin Doctors. Characters such as Peter Mandelson or Charlie Whelan revelled in their own mystique. Mandelson seemed to enjoy his nickname, 'The Prince of Darkness', so much that his later autobiography was advertised with him wearing a Dracula cape.

The '90s US sitcom Spin City had Mike Flaherty, the deputy mayor of New York, as the heroic protagonist, played by Michael J. Fox. Flaherty is the smart character surrounded by nincompoops, frequently using the dark arts to rescue situations and reputations.

Spin doctors became the subject of media attention; overexposed, investigated and reviled. The first line in the spin doctors' charter is 'never become the story'. If the spin doctor becomes more newsworthy than the stories they're selling, it's time for them to go. Charlie Whelan, with his briefings to journalists from the Red Lion pub, became more famous than the junior Treasury ministers of the day. Damian McBride, Gordon Brown's spin doctor, resigned after leaked emails suggested he wanted to smear Tory politicians with all kinds of vile untruths. Jo Moore resigned after it was revealed she had sent an email on 9/11 saying it was a good time to bury any bad news. Through the 1990s and into the 2000s, spin doctors were dragged from the darkness and into the media limelight. Their stories revealed a set of practices and a culture which most people found distasteful.

Over time, the term became debased and devalued, culminating in the fictional portrayal of Malcolm Tucker in Armando Iannucci's masterpiece The Thick of It. Tucker, the foul-mouthed, occasionally violent, government communications supremo is known as the 'Gorbals Goebbels', 'Iago with a BlackBerry' and has the 'physical demeanour and the political instincts of a velociraptor'. Tucker's method is a combination of threats and cajolery, backed by menace, and he brings down a Labour Party leader he is supposedly serving.

In 2011, the Danish political drama *Borgen* introduced us to Kasper Juul, the Prime Minister's spin doctor. We also learnt, pleasingly, that the Danish for 'spin doctor' is 'spin doctor'. Juul ends up as a political commentator and journalist, illustrating the well-trodden path taken by those who engage in politics later changing jobs to become those who talk about it.

In 2016, a French political thriller was broadcast. Its title in French was *Les Hommes de l'ombre*, which translates to 'The Men of the Shadows', a close cousin of Clare Short's famous denunciation of the 'men in the dark'. When shown on British TV, the title was replaced by a single word: 'Spin'.

WHAT IS A SPIN DOCTOR?

In fiction, spin doctors are crafty, manipulative, roguish and sly. The truth, as ever, is more mundane. Spin doctoring is a new expression of a very old practice. People with a story to tell have always tried to find the best way to tell it.

The world's religions depend on spin doctors – the priests, imams, vicars, rabbis and others who present their faith in the best possible light. Anyone trying to sell us something, from cars to holidays to cans of soup, needs to advertise the best features of their products. Anglers know a thing or two about spin – just ask them about the one that got away.

The ancient Greeks and Romans understood that the truth was not enough – it needed packaging and presentation, and so the art of rhetoric was developed.

Politicians, visionaries, revolutionaries, social reformers – all have used what today we caricature as spin. Lenin didn't sit at his desk in the Zurich public library and daydream about revolution – he created a newspaper with an army of spin doctors and sent them out to the Russian masses with his famous sound bite: 'bread, peace and land'. Florence Nightingale used the media to win support for extra supplies from a hard-hearted War Office. Even Jesus Christ knew a thing or two about communications – the need for eye-catching stunts, effective presentation, simple sound bites and memorable stories. He called them parables.

We all do it, all the time. From prehistoric times, the hunters retelling the story around the fire of their heroism in bringing down the biggest mammoth, to the people on Facebook telling us through their pictures and updates about their near-perfect lives, we accentuate the positive, and skip over the bad parts.

We do it when we apply for a job and face an interview panel, when we go on a date, when we try to sell our car or house, or when we meet someone for the first time. Like the market trader who puts the best apples at the front of their stall, we push forward the positive, the impressive, the interesting things about ourselves, and downgrade or ignore the negative. That's spin – seeking to influence others' opinions by the selection of information designed to create the right impression.

Spinning does not involve telling lies. If you lie on a first date, in a job interview, or when selling your house or car, the chances are you will be found out. If you lie on your job application to get a job, the employer can not only sack you if you are subsequently uncovered, they can sue you for damages. If you lie on a first date, well, it's not a relationship that's likely to last. If you lie to journalists, whatever the short-term advantage, you will be finished as a spin doctor.

Anyone serious about selling their message cannot rely on the occasional lunch with a newspaper editor or the odd news release. Building, maintaining and protecting a celebrity, corporate or political reputation is a full-time job, reflective of the insatiable demand for news and comment from an increasingly diverse media.

The explosive growth of the media means that there are more opportunities for spin: more news outlets that need more stories, more interview slots that need filling, more experts who need to share their insights, and more space for your message. The political parties' spin doctors need to pump out three or more stories a day, just to satisfy the beast. Like the plant in *Little Shop of Horrors*, the endless refrain is 'feed me'.

All of us can be spin doctors if we have a cause we want to promote, an issue we want to raise, or a campaign we want to kick-start. The techniques of the White House, Downing Street, St James's Palace and Square Mile spin doctors can be used to support the campaign to save the local hospital, sell tickets for the am-dram production of *The Mikado*, raise funds for the local scout troop, or plug a new charity, book or small business.

The reason is simple: the way we perceive the world beyond our personal experience is shaped by the media, the media is shaped by spin, and spin can be provided by you. What follows is not a guide to the black arts of manipulation and subterfuge, nor tips on lying and deceit, but some practical advice on how to influence the media in all its forms and get your message across.

If your voice deserves to be heard, neither an absence of knowledge about how to reach a wider audience via the media nor a lack of funds to hire a professional should be a barrier. This little book shows you how to be a spin doctor.

Chapter One

In Defence of Spin

If you've done it, it ain't braggin'.

—DIZZY DEAN, US BASEBALL PLAYER

ASK THE MAN or woman on the Clapham Omnibus about 'spin' and 'spin doctors' and you will receive a strongly negative reaction, as though you'd asked them about athlete's foot. Most people feel uneasy about the idea, and have it wrapped up in their minds with 'propaganda', 'manipulation', 'cheating', 'lying' and 'public relations'. Spin doctors are understood to be people who obfuscate, con, gossip and plot.

If you pursue the conversation and ask what it actually means, the same people fail to come up with a definition. People know spin is bad, but they don't know what it is. And if you ask people to name a spin doctor, they probably can't.

Melanie Phillips writing in *The Observer* on 12 October 1997, after just a few months of the Blair government, called spin doctoring 'a package of trickery, economies with the truth, manipulation of public credulity, bullying of journalists and favouritism'.

Michael Shea, who died in 2009, served as Her Majesty the Queen's spin doctor from 1978 to 1987. In 1986, he 'became the story' when fingers were pointed at him for briefing the *Sunday Times* that Her Majesty was not a big fan of the Prime Minister, Margaret Thatcher. After a mole-hunt it turned out Shea was the source, but he claimed to be misreported. In his political thriller *Spin Doctor* he describes these modern Machiavellis as 'professional political strategists, able on behalf of their clients to manipulate the media – planting a story here, a rumour there, a tip-off somewhere else – so that any piece of news is tailored to show them in the best possible light'.

We saw a dollop of this during the Labour Party's marathon reshuffle of the shadow front bench in January 2016, when anonymous 'sources' (people working for Jeremy Corbyn) briefed against Labour spokespeople for 'incompetence' and 'disloyalty'.

Another novelist, Ken Follett, goes further: 'People who do the briefing, who whisper words of poison into the ears of journalists, are of no consequence. They are the rent boys of politics, and we shudder with disgust when they brush past us in the corridor.'

The *Chambers 21st Century Dictionary* defines a spin doctor as 'someone, especially in politics, who tries to influence public opinion by putting a favourable bias on information presented to the public or to the media'.

The *Compact Oxford English Dictionary* suggests a spin doctor is 'a spokesperson for a political party or person employed to give a favourable interpretation of events to the media'.

These dictionary definitions get us some of the way there. It is right to highlight the realm of politics in the development of spin doctoring, but spin is far from confined to politicians. Most major organisations employ spin doctors: businesses, charities, celebrities, campaigns, even countries. We've known about the Queen's spin doctors for decades. What about the civil service, the Army, Waitrose, Virgin Atlantic, British American Tobacco, Facebook and the Stop the War Coalition – don't they employ spin doctors too? Don't Richard Branson, Kim Kardashian, Beyoncé, Eddie Redmayne and Adele employ spin doctors to look after their image? Of course they do.

And hang on a second. Wasn't our Prime Minister, David Cameron, once a spin doctor?

His future mother-in-law, Annabel Astor, persuaded Michael Green to take on Cameron as his director of corporate affairs at Carlton Communications. Cameron occupied this role from 1994 until 2001. He had never intended to stay there so long – he had believed John Major was going to call a general election in 1996. Unfortunately for Cameron, he failed to hold the traditionally Tory seat of Stafford in 1997 and thus was forced to return to Carlton to spin some more.

What about this idea of putting a 'favourable bias' or 'favourable interpretation' on information? Is putting a favourable bias on things confined to spin doctors? Who puts an unfavourable bias on what they say about themselves? With this definition, spin is no more morally reprehensible or responsible for the downfall of public standards than the used car salesman who gives his cars a good clean, or the job interviewee who selects their whitest shirt or blouse.

What about journalists? Don't they write and broadcast their own spin on things? Aren't the professional choices they make subject to their own convictions, views, prejudices, upbringing and proprietorial influence? Don't they choose to give a voice to certain points of view and perspectives which mirror their own view of the world, or the editorial line of their publication?

If journalists were simply reflectors of a perfect, objective truth, then the *Daily Mail* and *The Guardian* would be full of the same stories, written in the same way, every day of the week. Alastair Campbell wrote in the *Mirror* on 3 July 2000 that 'the vast bulk of spin comes from what I call journalist spin doctors'.

We don't have to go as far as the tinfoil-hat-wearing conspiracy theorists, the people who complain online about the 'MSM' (mainstream media) as the mouthpiece of an establishment plot to hide the truth. We should, however, recognise that journalists and media organisations have agendas.

The public, of course, understands this pretty well, and doesn't need someone in a Guy Fawkes mask to enlighten them.

The term 'spin doctor' was born, along with many of the techniques, in the United States of America. Spin doctor is an amalgam of 'spin' – the interpretation or slant placed on events (which is a sporting metaphor, taken from the spin put on a baseball by the pitcher, or the spin put on the cueball in pool), and 'doctor' deriving from the figurative uses of the word to mean 'patch up', 'piece together' and 'falsify'.

The phrase first appeared in print in the *New York Times* during the 1984 US Presidential elections, and during the '80s the term became common among the political classes on both sides of the Atlantic, especially during the 1988 US Presidential elections.

In Britain, the term is often applied to the handful of 'special advisers' employed by politicians. Special advisers are an important part of our machinery of government. Harold Wilson appointed the first ones, and every Prime Minister since has done the same. The numbers have steadily increased, despite opposition parties' calls to limit the numbers.

But not all special advisers are spin doctors. Most of the special advisers employed by government ministers are policy experts whose day-to-day work involves meetings with civil servants and interest groups, drafting policy documents and speeches, and providing another perspective and political advice to ministers otherwise reliant on the civil service. These special advisers have few, if any, dealings with the media beyond occasional phone briefings or ghost-writing articles.

Each Cabinet minister has a personal political spin doctor, and the Prime Minister has a handful. But the numbers are pitifully small compared to other systems, especially the fabled West Wing of the White House.

So what is a spin doctor? A spin doctor is a media specialist, with an expert knowledge and understanding of journalism and journalists, who uses his or her professional skill to help an organisation or individual get a message across to the right people.

It is a more highly skilled job, requiring a higher level of credibility and expertise, than a press officer or public relations officer. These jobs, though perfectly respectable and useful, are more concerned with drafting and issuing news statements, running social media accounts and answering factual enquiries from journalists.

The press officer is to the spin doctor what the first violin is to the orchestra's conductor. On this definition, it is obvious that spin doctors exist far beyond the narrow world of politics.

Wanted: Spin Doctor

'Wanted: Spin Doctor' is not a job ad you'll ever see.

The role is masked by other titles: head of communications, director of media, director of strategic communications, and so forth. But in my experience, the same attributes are required by all of these jobs, whatever the official job title may be.

The modern spin doctor must be in tune with all of the channels and platforms available, not just the traditional outlets of TV, radio, newspapers and magazines, but direct forms of communication such as Twitter, Instagram, Snapchat and Facebook.

He or she must have an instinctive feel for public opinion, but also be conversant with scientific methods of measuring how people think and feel about the world around them.

They must have great writing skills and be able to turn out speeches, press statements, policy briefings and tweets at a moment's notice, as well as ghost-writing anything from articles to books on behalf of their client.

Sometimes, experience of journalism is an advantage, but often the transition is hard and unsuccessful. Someone used to writing in their own name within a news organisation might find it hard to lead a team and work with others.

They must know a lot: about the area they're working in, the latest developments, thoughts and ideas, and what's around the corner. This involves spotting trends, analysing data, and having a sixth sense about how a media story might play out.

They must be resilient and self-confident: a lot of grief will come their way. They must be prepared to work over a 24-hour cycle, including weekends and public holidays, with little time for friends, family and sleep.

Lastly, they must be good company. Journalists must like and trust them. Senior figures must respect them. Their staff must admire them. They should be good at managing people.

Spin doctors are people employed for their skills at communicating. They can advise their bosses or organisations on how to present a positive face to the world, how to harness the awesome power of the mass media, how to avoid making the kind of mistakes which can send the share price into free-fall or cause the snap resignation.

The modern spin doctor is not a liar, or a dissembler, or a fraudster, or a manipulator – he or she is an invaluable asset to an organisation, and, much to the chagrin of journalists, an important contributor to the world of journalism. Journalists like to complain about spin doctors, especially if they're effective, but they rely on them in order to do their jobs.

The TV journalist Vincent Hanna once said that that the relationship between a politician and a journalist was that of a dog and a lamppost. He could just have easily been talking about spin doctors and journalists. I think that's an unfair characterisation. The relationship between a spin doctor and a journalist, if kept professional and based on some degree of trust, can be of mutual benefit. Journalists have to churn out stories, and people with a message have to sell it.

The spin doctor has become an invaluable link between leaders in business, politics and public life or celebrities and the consumers of media (that's you and me). It is through the media – newspapers, radio, television and internet – that we view the world beyond our immediate environment. In an age where few attend public meetings to hear speeches, or digest lengthy policy manifestos or a business prospectus, it is through the media that our reality is created.

We all like to think of ourselves as individuals, with our own distinct tastes, views, lifestyles and identity. Yet consider how much of your perception of the world comes through the prism of the media, not from personal experience. If I were to buy you a coffee and ask you for your opinion on any of the following:

- Jeremy Corbyn
- New Zealand
- The so-called Islamic State
- Ed Sheeran
- Hoxton

... I have no doubt that you'd have a view to share. But challenge yourself: how much of your view is based on personal experience, say bumping into Jeremy Corbyn and Ed Sheeran in a bar in New Zealand for example, and how much comes from the media?

What we experience directly is dwarfed by what we hear about from others. The truth is we largely form our perception of the world around us based on what we hear others say, often through newspapers, magazines, social media, websites, radio and TV. Your reality is shaped as much by that little screen in your pocket as the eyes and ears in your head.

Those who can use the media to their advantage can effectively shape reality.

The people employed in shaping this reality tend to work in communications or public relations for myriad organisations. The 2014 PR Census puts the number of people employed in PR in the UK at over 62,000 (PRCA, 2013).

The explosion of social media has enabled increasing numbers of companies to roll out a PR strategy in-house. This makes it difficult to gauge an accurate figure of the number of people employed in PR, but it's more than those working in coal-mining, iron, steel or any other of the industries which used to be the pillars of the British economy.

It is estimated there are around 4,200 PR agencies in the UK. In 2014, 62 per cent of firms reported increasing their digital and social media budget compared to the previous twelve months. There was a 13 per cent growth in the number of firms relying on their own social media efforts for PR rather than relying on an agency.

PR consultancies continue to turn over almost £10 billion a year – increasing by approximately 30 per cent in the last five years alone. Thirty-three UK universities and colleges offer PR as an undergraduate degree, with 140 different courses between them. PR is big business in the UK.

Public relations is a bigger activity than pure spin doctoring. Not all PRs are spin doctors.

THE TRUTH IS A DIFFICULT CONCEPT

If such a thing as absolute truth existed, there wouldn't be any spin doctors. But it doesn't, so there are. As Lord Justice Scott concluded at the completion of his inquiry into the Matrix Churchill scandal, 'the truth is a difficult concept'.

I'm not getting into the philosophical question of truth, which has occupied thinkers down the ages, from Aquinas to Wittgenstein. I merely make the point that what is considered to be true depends on a range of factors, from the source of the truth, the beliefs, convictions and prejudices of the recipients of the truth, the decade in which the truth was uttered, and so on. You can have a lot of fun marvelling at what intelligent people consider to be true, from astrology to the belief that 9/11 was faked.

This last belief, that the attacks on 9/11 were some kind of inside job, is promulgated by a growing industry of conspiracy theorists under the banner of the 9/11 truth movement. There's that word 'truth' again. There are plenty more 'truths' where that came from: that JFK was shot by more than a lone assailant; that aliens landed at Roswell, New Mexico; that NASA faked the moon landings; that Princess Diana was assassinated; that Paul McCartney died in the 1960s and was replaced by a lookalike; that the government scientist David Kelly was murdered by Iraqi secret agents; that the world is controlled by a secret world government.

Facts, figures, events, words: all have different meanings to different people. It all depends on perspective and interpretation. The internet, far from enhancing our understanding of the universe around us, has strengthened the role of interpretation and perspective.

As society's trust in 'experts' and professionals has diminished, individuals are bolstered by the half-baked, ill-informed and often entirely fictitious 'truths' that abound on the internet. People will earnestly repeat nonsense they've read on their phones as though they were sharing some great insight.

These falsehoods are often negative and can be hugely damaging to an individual or institution's reputation.

On social media, the truth can be shaped and spread within minutes, often with little relation to the facts. It can have catastrophic results, as with the case of the measles, mumps and rubella (MMR) vaccine. In 1998 a doctor called Andrew Wakefield published a study of twelve children with autism who had had the MMR vaccine. He established a link between the two, and soon tens of thousands of parents were refusing to get their children vaccinated. The rate of MMR vaccination dropped from 92 per cent to 80 per cent.

In 2010, the General Medical Council declared his research 'dishonest' and various medical bodies have shown there is no link between vaccines and autism. Yet parents persisted in their conviction, even when their children, and the children of others, were in danger. In 1998, there were fifty-six measles cases in the UK; by 2008, there were 1,348 cases, with two children tragically dying.

Over the past few years, a great number of viral news stories have been exposed as hoaxes. Social media allows these stories to spread rapidly; the pressure on the media to have the most up-to-date content means speed often takes precedence over verification.

There are 500 million tweets a day, 30 billion pieces of Facebook content a month, 300 hours of video uploaded to YouTube each second and news sites publishing and updating thousands of articles daily. We're all bombarded with more information than we can pause to verify or process.

In the early days of 24-hour TV news, the joke was that a story was 'never wrong for long'. The thirst to be first meant that broadcasters would get it wrong and quickly correct it afterwards. For example, broadcasters announced that Alan Johnson had been elected deputy leader of the Labour Party in 2007, when in reality it was Harriet Harman. This remained on the screen for a few seconds, before the broadcasters corrected their mistake.

The issue for social media is that an item may be shared countless times before verification. Once a tweet with false information is out in the ether, it belongs to the hive and may be retweeted thousands of times, regardless of the fact that it is wrong. Even if a correction soon follows, this might not be retweeted by the same people.

For example, an *Evening Standard* reporter once tweeted that 'Rio Ferdinand wins landmark privacy case against *Sunday Mirror*', when in fact he had lost. A correction was soon tweeted, but the original tweet is still out there in cyberspace, misinforming anyone who stumbles upon it.

Craig Silverman, a blogger on journalism, says: 'Social media is the most unverifiable information source in the world but the news media believes it because of its need for speed.'

In October 2014, the National Report website reported that street artist Banksy had been arrested in Watford. Within hours, all the main UK national newspapers featured the story on their websites. The original article contained multiple errors, including claims he had been arrested by the non-existent London Police and a quote from the Commissioner of the Metropolitan Police, 'Lyndon Edwards'. Presumably, Bernard Hogan-Howe (the actual Commissioner of the Met Police) was not particularly happy that no journalist recognised his role was being attributed to a fictional individual.

Perhaps the most common form of media to go viral is photography. In 2015, a photo appeared that seemed to show Ronald Reagan shaking hands with a young Vladimir Putin on a state visit in the mid-1980s. At this time, Putin was in fact in his thirties and a KGB agent.

Hoax news stories that go viral tend to tap into pre-existing anxieties among the general public about issues facing society. It's a mass form of 'confirmation bias' – we notice the things which back up our own views.

Here's a good example: in 2015, someone called Patrick tweeted a pie-chart of an opinion poll showing that 74 per cent of attendees of the Glastonbury festival had voted Conservative at the previous month's general election. It was mocked up to look like a *Guardian* poll, with *Guardian*-like colours and fonts (although not the actual font). It was gleefully retweeted by people who saw it as proof of their suspicions that Glastonbury had become mainstream, middle-class and commercial. These included *Guardian* journalists and, I'm ashamed to admit, myself. If we had thought about it for a moment, that figure of 74 per cent would have seemed ludicrously high. It confirmed our biases, and in a click it was retweeted.

Concerns about mass immigration have generated many scare articles in the tabloids attesting to the idea of immigrants taking over the UK. One such article in the *Daily Express* predicted the English language would die out. The Cabinet Office soon pointed out that the paper had misinterpreted – wilfully or not – the statistics, which measured the number of school pupils for whom English was not their first language. It offered no data about the number of UK school pupils who couldn't speak English at all. The *Express* was forced by IPSO to print a clarification on page two, refuting its earlier claims. Whether those who shared the article on social media were made aware of the clarification, however, is unknown and unlikely.

In 2015, *The Sun* claimed that a potential terrorist was able to travel from Turkey to Paris in six days, without a passport, by posing as a Syrian refugee. This assertion was based on the experience of reporter Emile Ghessen, who conducted this journey himself as an experiment.

What *The Sun* left out of their article was the fact that Ghessen had flown from Croatia to Paris on a British passport and thus had nothing on which to base his claim. *The Sun* later published an apology for their baseless reporting, by which point other national newspapers and the main UK news broadcasters had covered the story, reinforcing anti-refugee sentiment among the public.

Most of us have been left red-faced by sharing or commenting on viral news stories that have later been exposed as hoaxes. A celebrity death announced on Twitter is always treated with great caution, as these are often fake. Sometimes, the death is announced of a celebrity who has already died several years earlier. Tony Hart, the children's TV presenter, sadly died in 2009, but his death is announced and mourned regularly on Twitter.

When Margaret Thatcher died in 2013, pop fans on Twitter were devastated. Why? Because the hashtag #nowthatchers-dead made them believe singer Cher was dead. Some believed T. Hatcher was dead, dismaying the many fans of *Desperate Housewives* star Teri Hatcher. You need to careful with hashtags that can be read in different ways, as Susan Boyle's publicists discovered when they promoted her new collection of songs with the hashtag #susanalbumparty.

Pop fans were also saddened when comic Robin Williams died, because they thought it was Robbie Williams from Take That. Cue lots of sad references to 'angels'.

Hundreds of people recently retweeted an image of a service information notice at a Tube station that featured the hashtag #YouAintNoMuslimBruv. This followed video footage of the terrorist attack at Leytonstone Tube station where a bystander shouted the phrase to the perpetrator. It later emerged that the image had been generated digitally. Some of the viewers of the fake sign might have felt disappointed to discover the fakery; but most would have been unaware of the subsequent unveiling of the sign as a fake, and carry on to this day in the belief it was real. Thus 'the truth' is forged from digital fraud.

In the world of politics, you can find some of the most outrageous attempts to shape public views with a creative approach to the truth. A good example is the famous Liberal Democrat 'bar chart' used on election leaflets to show that the contest is a 'two-horse race' between whoever the leading party is and the Liberal Democrats. The 'facts' used to support this often spurious claim are usually not based on actual votes, or even opinion polls, but on numbers of councillors, votes in a local by-election, or some other flaky metric. The relative size of the bars on the bar chart usually bear little relation to the actual numbers.

There's a good Buzzfeed article headlined '15 Deeply Dubious Liberal Democrat Graphs' to give you a flavour, including the claim that it was a 'two-horse race' in Jeremy Corbyn's Islington North constituency. He won with a majority of over 20,000, and the Lib Dems came fourth.

Social media is unforgiving to politicians. It illuminates and amplifies their chance remarks and ill-considered thoughts. The *Telegraph* reported in November 2014 that: 'Labour was thrown into crisis after Mr Miliband was forced to sack Emily Thornberry from his shadow cabinet over a "contemptuous" tweet she posted of a house draped in the St George's Cross with a white van in the driveway.'

'Thrown into crisis', mark you.

Often, they are blamed for a slip-up by their aides. For example, Ed Miliband was lampooned for the following gaffe, but I doubt he was anywhere near his Twitter account at the time of the crime, as reported here in the *Telegraph* in January 2012:

Ed Miliband red-faced after 'Blackbuster' Twitter gaffe

Ed Miliband, the Labour leader, has bungled the simple task of sending a tweet to mark the death of Bob Holness, the host of Blockbusters.

Mr Holness died peacefully in his sleep early this morning aged 83.

A message posted from Ed Miliband's Twitter account read: 'Sad to hear that Bob Holness has died. A generation will remember him fondly from Blackbusters.'

The message was hastily deleted, and re-written to correctly refer to the 1980s trivia quiz as 'Blockbusters'.

In April 2016, Jeremy Corbyn was mocked for tweeting that he had met 'the Barack Obama' (as opposed to all the other Barack Obamas). Again, it is unlikely Corbyn made the error. It was almost certainly an over-enthusiastic aide.

So the truth is indeed a difficult concept, made all the murkier by social media. As the socialist MP Aneurin Bevan used to challenge his interlocutors: 'This is my truth, now tell me yours.'

Chapter Two

Why Bother?

A good reputation is more valuable than money.

—Publius Syrus (First century BC)

W HY SHOULD ANYONE bother? Hasn't all this obsession with style, spin and packaging gone too far? If the product you're selling is decent, or the message you're telling is authentic, surely people will take you at face value? Isn't there a thirst for keeping it real? For that most attractive of all attributes, authenticity? Aren't people intelligent enough to make up their own minds, without a coat of varnish and a load of old blather?

Nope.

YOUR REPUTATION MATTERS

Your reputation matters. It shapes how others perceive you, whether they want to do business with you, or give you their money, or vote for you, or work for you. It determines whether they'll give you the benefit of the doubt if you do something stupid, and whether they believe you if you say you're sorry. It's a valuable asset, and it needs polishing and looking after. You can't control your reputation, only influence it by what you do and say. On one level, it shouldn't matter what people say about you, if you are psychologically robust and feel comfortable in your own skin. On another level, it matters a great deal because it determines your social, financial and professional success.

Spin doctors are employed to shape reputations – of individuals and institutions. They do this by understanding public sentiment and by being plugged into the popular mood. They know how information will be received by journalists, and then by the public, and how it shapes their clients' reputations. They have faith in the public's good sense, and that people can sniff out a fake or a phoney.

No amount of spin can save you if your reputation crashes and burns. Even the mighty Coca-Cola came a cropper when it tried to introduce Dasani bottled water into the UK market. Dasani is a successful brand in many countries. It is purified water, with some minerals added. But it comes from the tap. When Coke started bottling up tap water and selling it to British consumers for a pound a bottle they might have assumed all would be well. However, *The Grocer* magazine broke the news that the water had not trickled from an Alpine stream but poured from a tap, and soon the rest of the media joined in the outrage. It wasn't helped by an episode of *Only Fools and Horses*, which had shown Del Boy and Rodney flogging 'Peckham Spring' water which they'd got from Thames Water. Five weeks after the launch, Dasani disappeared from the shelves, its reputation sunk forever.

If we're operating in the commercial world, reputation is everything. The growth in online review websites means reputations can be made and broken with the tap of a keyboard. Sites such as TripAdvisor shape the reputations of restaurants, hotels and even whole cities. They change not only the way we think, but the way we behave. It's a strong-minded person who will knowingly book into a hotel with a string of stinking online reviews.

HOW TO EARN A GOOD REPUTATION

A good reputation is like a reservoir of water, built up over time with every drop of rain. Each transaction you or your organisation undertake, every time you delight someone, rescue a situation or go the extra mile, you add to your store of reputation. To extend the reservoir metaphor, if the water level is high, then if the dam is breached there's enough water left. If the water level is low to start with, the reservoir runs dry. If something goes wrong, your reputation will hang in the balance. If you've protected and nurtured your reputation

over the years, people will give you the benefit of the doubt
– depending, of course, on the severity of the transgression!

Very few people, with the possible exception of military or
sporting heroes, build a reputation on a single act. Most of
us build a reputation on the thousand and one things we do
well. The same is true of institutions, organisations and companies: every email replied to, every phone call taken, every
apology and every ounce of empathy will add to the store of
your good reputation.

Reputation is something which needs to be refreshed and
replenished. You can't rely on past glories. In most businesses
you're only as good as your last review.

There's a story attributed to the American politician Alben
William Barkley (1877–1956). Barkley, standing for some
office or other, encountered a once-loyal voter who claimed
he was contemplating voting for the other candidate.

Barkley reminded him of the many things he had done for
him as prosecuting attorney, as county judge, as congressman
and as senator.

He recalled how he had helped get an access road built to
his farm, how he had visited him in a military hospital in France
when he was wounded in the First World War, how he had assis-
ted him in securing his veteran's benefits, how he had arranged
his loan from the Farm Credit Administration, how he had got
him a disaster loan when a flood destroyed his home.

'How can you think of voting for my opponent?' he exhorted
at the end of this long recital. 'Surely you remember all these
things I have done for you?'

'Yeah,' said the voter, 'I remember. But what in hell have you done for me lately?'

A spin doctor knows a reputation must be constantly nourished with new stories and pictures. You can't rest on your laurels. The public will justifiably ask *what have you done for me lately?*

HOW TO DESERVE A BAD REPUTATION

There are numerous ways to gain a bad reputation. You can do lots of things badly over time, or one big thing badly all at once. You can be Fawlty Towers, dismaying and disappointing your customers with random acts of incompetence, or you can be BP in the Gulf of Mexico, spilling 4.2 million barrels of oil into the sea, and ending up paying out £12 billion in fines.

Often it is the actions of the leaders in a crisis which determine how the organisation is perceived. Leaders become lightning rods. Tony Hayward, CEO of BP, became the most hated man in America following the oil spill. People weren't happy with all the oil, but they were even less pleased with the gaffes that followed, such as his claim that the spill was 'relatively tiny' compared with the 'very big ocean', his remark in an interview that 'I'd like my life back' and the fact that he took a day off to go sailing in the middle of the crisis.

During floods in the UK in 2015, the head of the Environment Agency, Sir Philip Dilley, decided to mastermind the response from home, which unfortunately happened to be in Barbados. He ended up resigning. His departure is a great example of the power of perception. To my knowledge, they have phones and Wi-Fi in Barbados. Sir Philip, as part-time chair of the agency, was not expected to turn up to flood-stricken parts of Yorkshire and start diverting rivers. Whatever his role, he could do it from Barbados as easily as Todmorden. But he failed the basic test of public opinion, as any good spin doctor could have warned him.

THE GRANDDADDY OF THEM ALL: DOING A RATNER

The case of Gerald Ratner stands out in the annals of communications cock-ups. It is cited so often for two reasons. First, the reputation-destroying act itself was over in a matter of seconds, and entirely avoidable. Second, the impact was thermo-nuclear, leaving nothing standing in its wake.

The story runs like this. Gerald Ratner was an incredibly successful businessman who started life as a market trader in Petticoat Lane. He built a chain of high-street jewellery shops, using a range of discounts, vouchers and high-powered sales and marketing techniques.

Ratner described his business as making jewellery accessible to the masses, in same way as eating out, or discount long-distance flights had become. When the 42-year-old Ratner stood up to address the annual convention of the Institute of Directors (IoD) in 1991 at the Royal Albert Hall, he was a business leader at the top of his game. He wore a smart dark suit, light striped shirt, and dark grey tie.

He told his story with confidence and humour. His business controlled 34 per cent of the jewellery market, with over 1,000 shops in the UK and 1,000 in the US. The day before his speech, Ratner Group had announced, in the depths of recession, a profit of £120 million. His shops made more money per square foot than any other shops in Europe.

The famous line in the speech concerned one of his best-selling items, a sherry decanter, tray and glasses which retailed at £4.95. Even back in 1991, that wasn't much money. In a rhetorical flourish, Ratner asked how he could make such profits on goods that cost so little. He answered himself with the line: because it's 'total crap'. As his audience laughed and applauded him, he added by way of codicil, 'There's no point beating around the bush.'

Total crap.

Never have two words had such a calamitous impact on a business.

The tabloid newspapers leapt on his remarks and asked his customers what they thought. The response was instant. And consider that this was in the analogue days when a news story had a day-long cycle. £500 million was wiped off the value of the company within days. The company was the same company, with the same premises, staff, goods and leadership. Yet the collapse of its reputation meant it was worth £500 million less.

Sales dropped. Profits slumped. Today, there are no Ratners on the high street. They have vanished like the shine on a crappy gold-plated necklace that cost less than a Marks & Spencer prawn sandwich.

Like many people in the world of communications, I've been telling the story of Gerald Ratner for years, but it was only recently that I watched the actual speech on YouTube. It is twenty-five minutes long, and it is actually rather impressive. The overall theme is that despite all the sneers and snobbery, Ratners was successful because it gave people what they wanted. It may have been a bit rough around the edges, like its founder, but it brought gold into the lives of millions of people who otherwise would never afford it. In the 1980s if you wanted gold earrings for 99 pence, there was only one place to go, and that was Ratners.

The story of Gerald Ratner is a morality tale about the dangers of hubris. It demonstrates the often imperceptible value of reputation, and how an organisation rests on its foundations. Once fatally damaged, it was impossible to rebuild.

It also serves as a reminder to 'sense check' every line of every piece of communication, whether it's a tweet, speech, brochure or website, in case you've inadvertently offended your audience. If you insult the people who pay your wages, you should not be too surprised if the reaction is swift and brutal.

HOW TO CREATE A STRATEGY

Once a leader or public figure has arrived at the decision to manage their reputation and not just leave it to chance, they need to create a strategy. That's where the spin doctor comes in. A spin doctor must have a strategic brain, as well as a grasp of tactics. A spin doctor's life comprises a series of sporadic activities – phone calls, texts, tweets, tapping out copy – but unless they are part of a bigger plan, they may lack cohesion.

First, you need to be clear why you're engaging in communications in the first place. All communication seeks to change either our opinions, or our actions, or both. Advertising people understand this: they may enjoy winning awards for creativity, but they won't have any clients if their ads don't shift products.

Spin doctoring is no different in this regard. You need to be clear what you want people to think, and what you want them to do. In politics, the end result comes on polling day and whether people vote for you or not.

The template for a strategy might look like this:

Why are we doing this? What do we want to achieve?

Link the communications to the organisation's overall aims.
That might be campaigning for change, fundraising, winning
elections or selling goods and services. Be clear that media
coverage is not an end in itself, no matter how laudatory.
It must be linked back to a plan.

What are we saying? What's our message?

Start with your 'narrative' – the 500-word story of what you're
all about and what you want to achieve. This is where you frame
your argument.

Then decide on some 'key messages', the things you want people to know. The US strategist Frank Luntz points out that the way you describe things can influence how we perceive them. 'Drilling for oil' sounds negative, compared to 'energy exploration', which sounds positive. Campaigners against what the government calls the 'spare room subsidy' describe it as a 'bedroom tax', which sounds wholly negative. Finally, work out your sound bites: the short, sharp, compelling and repeatable phrases that will run through all your communications. They might be as simple as Barack Obama's 'Yes We Can'. Once you've agreed all this, stick to it. Stay 'on message'.

How will we say it? What channels will we select?
Everyone's default is Twitter because it's fast and reaches thousands, but don't ignore the range of other media. The more times a message appears across different media, the more impact it has. Amplify your message across many different media. Don't forget Marshall McLuhan's famous concept: the medium is the message. If you want to be taken seriously, go for the *Financial Times*. If you want to look like a tribune of the people, go for the *Mirror*.

Who will say it? Who are our advocates and spokespeople?
You need a spokesperson who people trust and like. They might not be the most senior person. They might not even be someone who is directly associated with you. Sometimes, the best spokespeople are 'third parties' who can endorse you with authenticity. In a crisis, you need 'experts'.

Who is our audience? What are they reading and listening to?
The issue with social media is that it creates a terrible echo
chamber. People hear what they want to hear because of who they
follow. You need to reach beyond a merry band of followers to the
people who can influence your chances of success. This requires
segmentation of the audience, and a forensic understanding of
their media habits. The starting point is that the people you need
to reach are unlikely to be anything like you. There are still people
in the world who get their news the day after it happens.

**When will we say it? What's the optimum time to get
our message across?**
You need to plan a grid of activities. A grid is a system of
issues and activities, with target outlets mapped against time.
It comprises a day-to-day calendar, with a diary of events,
announcements and activities mapped across it. In a complex
organisation, it allows spin doctors to spread out their activity,
to avoid both clashes and gaps in activity, stretching out like a
desert. Governments work to a grid so that Cabinet ministers
are not making big announcements on the same day, competing
for the same airtime.

How will we adapt if it doesn't work?
If it looks like it isn't working, you need to stop banging your head
against the wall, and try something else.

The most important thing about your strategy is to write
it down, and agree upon it across the whole organisation.

As the much-missed Labour strategist Philip Gould used to say: 'If it's not written down, it doesn't exist.'

The day-to-day tactics are down to the skill and judgement of the spin doctor. They should have some operational freedom, but it should be set against the context of a broader strategy that everyone has signed up to. There is no room for mad dogs.

Chapter Three

Understanding the Modern Media

*Many people would no more think of entering journalism than
the sewage business – which at least does us all some good.*

—STEPHEN FRY

S PIN DOCTORS MUST understand the media and the
people who work in it. You have to be an avid consumer of news, to enjoy great journalism, to watch a
big television interview as some people watch a football match, and to revel in great writing.

To be a successful spin doctor you must know what gets journalists' juices flowing, and conversely, what makes them want to slam the phone down. You have to be able, in the words of Harper Lee, to stand in their shoes and walk around.

That's why some (but not all) former journalists make effective spin doctors: because they understand the structure and culture of the modern media. Few were surprised when David Cameron appointed the former editor of the *News of the World* Andy Coulson as his spin doctor, or when Jeremy Corbyn appointed *The Guardian*'s comment editor Seumas Milne. Margaret Thatcher appointed Bernard Ingham, who had started out aged sixteen as a reporter on the *Hebden Bridge Times*, and had been a reporter on the *Yorkshire Post*. Harold Wilson appointed the *Mirror*'s political editor Joe Haines. Thirty years later, Tony Blair appointed the *Mirror*'s political editor Alastair Campbell. It's a well-trodden path.

The most important attribute for the spin doctor is to understand journalists and the organisations they work for: what motivates them, what excites them, what annoys them and the pressures of the job that they suffer.

It is also vital to understand the news-gathering process and the structure and machinery of the modern media. You need to appreciate how the digital revolution is changing the media industry, and shaping how we consume our news and views. You have to be able to talk the same language.

THE STRUCTURE OF THE MEDIA

The 'media' is not a single entity, except in the heads of people who think in terms of conspiracies; it comprises organisations big and small, from the mighty BBC with its 2,000 journalists all over the world, to the tiniest local paper with one writer, and relies on people turning up to work and doing their jobs, plus a growing army of contractors and freelances. Like every industry, the media industry is undergoing huge change.

When I tell people I did work experience on my local paper, the *Buckinghamshire Advertiser*, in the mid-1980s, they are usually incredulous when I say the copy was typed on big typewriters, with carbon paper to make three copies, the pages were laid out using bits of metal, and the photographs were developed in a dark room using acetic acid and ammonium thiosulphate.

When I was there in 1985, the Beaconsfield reporter was David Yelland, who went on to become editor of *The Sun*. The newsroom of the *Buckinghamshire Advertiser*, with its sweary journalists, piles of paper, clattering typewriters and general inkiness, would have been immediately recognisable to ex-journalist Charles Dickens.

Even a couple of years later when I edited my university student magazine, the technology was rudimentary. There was a single Apple Macintosh computer in its own special room (the 'Mac Room') on which the lucky few could perform 'desk-top publishing'. The pages were still cut and pasted using a scalpel and spray glue, and printed with ink on huge printing machines.

Since the 1980s, the technology of news-making has transformed. The only legacy of the newspaper industry in Fleet Street, aside from a few signs above buildings like the one for the *Dundee Courier*, is the preponderance of pubs and wine bars.

SO WHAT DOES THE MODERN MEDIA LOOK LIKE?

A successful spin doctor should understand how the modern media is structured. This allows them to enter the world and thought-processes of the journalists they deal with, and also to appreciate how their target audiences are receiving their news. A piece in *The Times* is useless if the people you want to persuade are reading Buzzfeed.

The big shift is the digital revolution. Newspapers are now online news entities which produce paper versions of their product. In a few years' time, many will be purely online, delivering constantly updated news and views to your device of choice. Many magazines have already gone down this road, publishing only online.

The modern journalist is churning out more copy than ever, not just a main story and some NIBs (News in Brief), but also endless updates to online content, live blogs of unfolding stories, content for frequent tweets on Twitter, and audio and visual content for podcasts.

It won't be long before we stop talking about 'social media', just as we've stopped talking about 'new media'. It's all just 'the media'. This allows spin doctors more opportunities than ever to shape and steer a story as it develops, and to inject material directly into the bloodstream of a story through their own controlled media such as Twitter, YouTube or Facebook.

A survey by the Chartered Institute for Public Relations (CIPR) in January 2016 asked top public relations practitioners: 'Which three channels were most important for you in communicating key messages in the last three months?'

The results were:

- Twitter: 61 per cent
- Print: 54 per cent
- Facebook: 38 per cent

With other channels such as email, events, TV, radio, and social media such as Snapchat, YouTube, LinkedIn, Vine and Instagram coming below. The point here is that, whereas a story running on the Guido Fawkes website may feel like a big deal for those in the eye of the storm, the impact on public opinion will still be felt hardest if the story gets into national, and local, newspapers.

How do we consume our media? The UK media can be broken down into sectors:

- National newspapers
- Television
- Radio
- Online

The obvious observation here is the blurring of the lines between the sectors and the blending of different media as technology develops. Whereas once, the television dominated the living room, with all the furniture pointing towards it, and all the family members watching EastEnders (viewed by 30 million on Christmas Day 1986) or the Morecambe and Wise Show (the 1977 Christmas special was viewed by 28 million people), today the scene is different.

The TV is more likely to be hooked up to a games console while each family member watches their own choice of programmes on a tablet or phone. Mum and Dad can watch War and Peace on iPlayer while the kids watch videos on YouTube. EastEnders remains one of the programmes with the highest audience figures, but that's only eight million people, far fewer than they had in 1986.

NATIONAL NEWSPAPERS

When we talk of the 'press', we think of national newspapers. The national newspapers still carry huge authority and influence, and contain the best, and worst, of British journalism. For every warm and witty Alan Coren, or erudite and wise Christopher Hitchens, there is a journalist going through the bins of celebrities, looking for pregnancy-testing kits.

In the Victorian era, the Pall Mall Gazette's campaign, led by William Stead, highlighted the sexual abuse of young people on London's streets and led to the passing of new laws to protect them. Stead said journalism is 'a very good way of attacking the devil'. He later died in the Titanic disaster, having given his life jacket to another passenger.

In the 1970s, Harry Evans's Sunday Times led the campaign to expose the plight of the victims of thalidomide. Hundreds of children were born without arms and legs, or blind, because of a drug their mothers were prescribed during pregnancy. The pharmaceutical company responsible attempted initially to deny responsibility. Thanks to Harry Evans, there was eventually some compensation. It remains one of the worst scandals and cover-ups of the twentieth century.

In one of those nice coincidences, William Stead, campaigning in the 1880s, and Harry Evans, campaigning a century later, both built their careers as editors of the Northern Echo newspaper in Darlington. Newspapers can be a powerful force for good, as well as news, views and entertainment.

Great names of literature including Charles Dickens, George Orwell, Rudyard Kipling, Ian Fleming and Jack London began as journalists. Most newspapers have long, illustrious pedigrees. Most of us read one, either as a paper or online, and many of us identify with one of them as 'our' newspaper.

The demise of the News of the World in 2011, after bringing murders, scandals and celebrities into our Sunday mornings since 1843, proves that no newspaper, no matter how established, has an automatic right to exist.

Ninety per cent of British adults (aged fifteen and over) read newspapers on an average weekday, according to the National Readership Survey. Sixty-nine per cent of these adults read a print newspaper, while 72 per cent access news content online.

The number of adults reading print newspapers has actually risen by 10 per cent in the last forty years, after years of decline. This increase in the proportion of adults reading print newspapers is down to the free titles available on public transport across the UK. With 3.2 million estimated daily readers, the *Metro* is the main publication of this type.

Metro provides political, financial and celebrity news alongside comment and opinion pieces for free to its readers. Similarly, the *Evening Standard*, while technically a regional paper, spreads across the south-east and beyond on commuter trains, reaching over 1.7 million readers a day.

It's not just the *what* of journalism that has transformed, it is also the *how*. Gone are the days when a newspaper was delivered to your door and consumed over the breakfast table. While twenty years ago most people would buy the same title every day, the ability to access news websites, largely for free, means we can utilise a wide variety of news sources throughout the day.

For example, we might buy a copy of *The Times* to read on our morning commute, peruse different publications' websites during our lunch break, scan Twitter in our mid-afternoon break, read the *Metro* on our journey home and have another scan of Twitter during *Newsnight* for commentary.

The reach of newspapers has increased dramatically. It means that *The Sun* is no longer confined to *Sun* readers, nor *The Guardian* to *Guardian* readers. Stories, if they have legs, can run across titles and platforms, reaching audiences way beyond their traditional readerships. You can read a funny story in *The Australian* or a heart-breaking tale in the *Washington Post* as easily as in your local paper.

This makes it less important to think about where you place a story or article, because if it's strong enough, it will be spread across social media. An article in the Huffington Post can reach your target audience, if you use Twitter and Facebook to push it.

There are eleven national daily newspapers, twelve if we include the freesheet *Metro*. They can be divided into 'pops', 'red tops' or tabloids ('tabs'): (*Sun, Mirror, Daily Star*), mid-markets (*Express, Daily Mail*) and the broadsheets and compacts (*Guardian, Times, Financial Times, Daily Telegraph* and the *i.*) There is also Jeremy Corbyn's favourite the *Morning Star*, which follows the line of the Communist Party of Britain (based in Croydon), and which inexplicably you can buy in WH Smith.

Added to these are the national Sunday newspapers: *Sun on Sunday, Sunday Mirror, Daily Star Sunday, Mail on Sunday, People, Sunday Times, Express on Sunday, Sunday Telegraph* and *The Observer*.

Readerships vary greatly between these newspapers. *The Sun* is read by around twelve and a half million people every day (Press Gazette, 2015). The *Financial Times* sells around 214,000 copies a day, mostly outside the UK (Press Gazette, 2015). *The Times* and *Sunday Times* have about 140,000 subscribers paying for their digital content. I chaired a seminar a couple of years ago with a delegation from a Chinese regional newspaper. To them, these circulation figures seemed so laughably small, they checked that the translator hadn't got the numbers wrong.

Newspapers have their own political slant: the *Mirror* is broadly Labour, the *Daily Telegraph* is mostly Tory. After 1997, *The Guardian* and *Daily Mail* were both visceral in their loathing of the Labour government, but for entirely different reasons: the latter because they considered the Blair government too left wing, and the former because it wasn't left wing enough.

A financial spin doctor will target the FT because of the kind of people who read it (business leaders, investors), rather than the number of readers. Political spin doctors recognise the value of mass circulation tabloids like *The Sun* for spreading a political message to millions. When they want to communicate subtler messages to their own parties, they might choose newspapers which are read by party supporters.

An article placed in *The Guardian* will reach most of the Labour Party membership, despite that newspaper's hostility to the Labour Party. Similarly, whenever the Tories have something to say to Tories, they tend to choose the *Daily Telegraph* as their 'house journal'. Then an enterprising spin doctor will try to reach beyond their core support by getting a Tory Cabinet minister to write for *The Guardian*, or a Labour frontbencher to write for the *Telegraph*.

The dilemma for newspapers' owners is how to make money from all this cross-pollinated, easy-access content. Attempts at subscription models have not been successful. Most people can pick up a free newspaper every weekday, or read news stories on their phone at any time, so why spend money on something you can have for free? The dash to digital has helped the consumer, but not the owners.

REGIONAL AND LOCAL PAPERS

Local newspapers are more important than you might think. There are over 100 daily local and regional newspapers and 1,300 weeklies in the UK. The most popular across the UK are the *Wolverhampton Express and Star*, *Manchester Evening News*, *Liverpool Echo*, *Shropshire Star*, *Newcastle Evening Chronicle*, *Glasgow Evening Times*, *Leicester Mercury* and the *Stoke Sentinel*.

If you're one of those people who complains that 'they're all adverts' then you should be asking why so many advertisers pay hard cash to place ads. It's not for love. It's because local papers are read by enough people to make advertising worthwhile. Local weekly and daily newspapers attract over £2 billion of advertising revenue per year (only television attracts more) and over 80 per cent of adults read their local paper. Forty per cent of adults claim to prefer their local paper to the nationals.

Regional and local newspapers have suffered in recent years, with reductions in advertising revenue, numbers of staff and readers. Often the smaller titles are staffed by just one or two news journalists, making them great targets for spin doctors. The journalists tend to be young, first- or second-jobbers, and keen to make their mark. Most stay on the paper for only a year or two, and most dream of a job on a national newspaper.

If your targeting is right, your story has a strong local angle, and your news release is well-written, you have a good chance of success. Sometimes your words will appear verbatim, a phenomenon known as 'churnalism'. I once sent a news release to a freesheet which not only printed the text word-for-word, but also the news release instructions to the subs including 'ends' and 'for more information contact Paul Richards...'.

The local angle is the key, though. If the story is about an event in the wrong part of town or the wrong village (off 'the patch'), the journalist won't touch it. Elvis Presley could be sighted, aliens could land, Shergar might be chewing grass on the village green, but if it's off the patch, a local paper won't cover it.

Local papers want a steady diet of local stories about local people, events or places. Local campaigns and pressure groups can do well, or local interest groups like the local history society, local hospital league of friends, and local teams and clubs.

MAGAZINES

There has been an explosion of titles in the magazine sector in the last twenty years. In the last decade, the number of magazines produced has increased by a third, and circulation has increased by over 10 per cent. Magazines are now available for every leisure and lifestyle interest, from women's mags like

Cosmopolitan, Elle, Glamour, Good Housekeeping, Red and Woman's Own, to consumer titles like BBC Good Food Magazine, Radio Times and Which?.

There are also current affairs and political magazines which reach important audiences, like the New Statesman, Spectator, and The Economist. The top-selling magazines such as Take a Break have readerships in the millions.

The lead times for publication in a magazine may be months. The approach you make is very different from contacting a newsroom. Magazines use freelancers for much of their material, and so the relationship you need to develop with the journalist is harder to pin down. If you want to place stories and features in magazines, you need to plan months in advance and place material which suits the style and content of the target title.

The benefit of having your message appear in lifestyle and consumer magazines is that people tend to be less cynical and sceptical about what they read there. A serious message which appears in a consumer mag has greater reach, and therefore greater impact, than one which appears in a 'serious' magazine such as The Economist. Political parties have begun to target these titles, especially women's magazines, because they can reach audiences in ways which traditional news media have exhausted.

In the run-up to the 2015 general election, all four of the main party leaders gave interviews with multiple lifestyle magazines: David Cameron (Woman and Home, Red, Heat); Ed Miliband (Red, Cosmopolitan, Now); Nick Clegg (Stylist, GQ,

Good Housekeeping) and Nicola Sturgeon (GQ, Grazia, Vogue). The focus of these interviews was the human side of the party leaders, their family lives, interests and, in Nick Clegg's case, his number of past sexual partners.

TRADE AND TECHNICALS

These tend to appear as the 'joke' title in the missing words round of Have I Got News for You, but for many thousands of journalists, publications like British Baker and Dairy Farmer are their bread and butter.

Amateur Gardening, Angling Times, Bee World, Bird Watching, The Budgerigar, Flying Saucer Review, Freemasonry Today, The Grocer, Helicopter International, Local Historian, Manchester United Magazine, Materials Recycling World, Municipal Journal, Office Supplies News, Packaging Week, Pig Farming, Rugby World, Shoe and Leather News, Sporting Gun, Structural Engineer, Timber Trades Journal, Water Bulletin, Which Motorcaravan, Your Cat and finally Zionist Review are magazines which delight, amuse and make the day of millions of people. These titles are also eagerly awaited by thousands of people in the relevant business or trade, as a source of unique information and news.

They can be the source of news stories for the nationals and broadcasters. A health story might break in The Lancet, a political story in The Spectator, or a science story in New Scientist.

BROADCAST

Television

In terms of mass communication, television is the most powerful medium – that's why advertisers spend millions to promote their products on TV. Spin doctors take TV very seriously indeed because of this potency. Ninety-nine per cent of UK households have a TV set, 64 per cent have two and 28 per cent have three or more. Forty per cent of leisure time is spent watching TV. A visual image is far more powerful than the printed word.

In our times, television has undergone a revolution. From the days when TV meant a choice of three channels, today people can access thousands. We have seen, since the '80s, the launch of Channel Four, Channel Five, breakfast TV, the introduction of cable and satellite, 24-hour news programmes, countless sports channels and specialist channels on every topic from nature to history to cooking.

The proliferation of channels has meant there are many more opportunities for spin doctors. Stations like Sky News, Al Jazeera, the BBC News channel and cable channels have a great deal of airtime to fill. They have an insatiable appetite for talking heads, and can be targeted for interviews and comment. All news channels have a programme focused on analysis of the day's newspapers. These offer an opportunity for the politician or company representative to discuss current affairs and pro-mote their party, charity or business in a fairly relaxed setting.

Television news programmes remain the best target for spin doctors; the daily bulletins are monitored closely by the political parties, and producers are phoned if they sense any bias or omissions. The most important are the 6.30 p.m. ITN news and the 6 p.m. BBC news bulletins, and then the 10 p.m. BBC and 10 p.m. ITN bulletins. These news programmes are known in the business by the times they start. You should refer to 'the Ten' or the 'the Six' if you want to sound like you know what you're talking about.

You can occasionally spot the spin by following the progress of a particular story on these bulletins during a day. The coverage may change from lunch-time to tea-time, to evening as the story develops, new interviews are edited in, new angles appear, and the spin doctors have gone to work. The local television stations have local news operations which can be targeted with good local stories with plenty of visual interest.

The digital expansion of television means there are now many more programmes on TV and much more content to produce. Thus, it is no longer unusual to see politicians appearing on *Saturday Kitchen*, *GMB* or even *Celebrity Big Brother* (though the last example should probably be avoided if George Galloway's experience is anything to go by).

Radio

Like television, the structure of the radio industry is split between the BBC and the commercial sector, and organised on a national and local level.

The BBC has prestige programmes like *Today* and *The World at One (WATO)*, which set the news agenda and reach important opinion-forming audiences.

The country is covered in local radio stations. Each major town has a BBC station and one or more commercial stations. All radio stations carry an element of news. The forty BBC local radio stations use news fed from the national operation, and from their own news desks. They are supplied material from the GNS (the General News Service), which makes live interviews available to a range of local stations one after the other, from a single studio.

Commercial radio uses its own reporters and Independent Radio News (IRN), based at the ITN headquarters. Stations like Talk Radio, Radio Five Live and LBC rely on a constant supply of interviewees and thus are a good target for getting on air. Local radio needs local stories with the same criteria as local papers – with the obvious exception that radio needs people to talk about the story.

The smaller digital stations have very few staff, especially at the weekends, and so it is important to make the right approach. There is a world of difference between phoning at five minutes to the hour, when the news presenter is desperately finishing off scripts for the hourly news bulletin, and five minutes after the hour, when the bulletin is over and the presenter has time to talk to you.

ONLINE

The rise of digital media has not only challenged and changed the way the traditional media works and is organised, it has also created myriad new platforms for news and views.

In the regular lists of top UK websites, based on the number of people interacting with them, the following sites usually appear:

- Google
- Facebook
- YouTube
- Amazon
- eBay
- BBC Online
- Yahoo!
- Windows Live
- Wikipedia
- Twitter
- LinkedIn
- Lad Bible
- Mail Online
- PayPal
- Guardian

The Guardian, Mail and BBC dominate the online market for news, but look at how sites with content generated by their

users – Twitter, YouTube, LinkedIn, Facebook, Wikipedia
– are up there. No spin doctor can rely on journalists for
their 'earned media' (coverage they generate by creating
compelling news stories). Today, you need to be creating your own media, via your own channels, direct to your
audiences.

An article on the Huffington Post, an interview on
Mumsnet, an amusing mention on Buzzfeed: these things
can matter as much as to your reputation as a favourable
mention in *The Times'* leader.

NEWS AGENCIES

A news agency is a news-gathering organisation which sells
its news and information to print and broadcast media.
National and international agencies such as the Press Association (PA), Associated Press, Bloomberg Business News
or Reuters serve newsrooms and other organisations via
an online link-up, still known as a 'wire'. 'What's running
on the wires?' means 'What stories are appearing from the
news agencies?'.

Smaller agencies might specialise in subject areas such
as sport or courts reporting, or be based on a specific geographical area (for example, Bournemouth News and Picture
Service, Anglia Press Agency). The National Association of
Press Agencies (NAPO) has a directory of all these local and
national agencies.

The Press Association (PA) is the main news agency in the UK, jointly owned by the national newspapers. It has a vital role in the creation of news, and is therefore of great importance in the world of spin doctoring. The Press Association is not a media outlet in its own right – it supplies news stories and information to newsrooms.

PA has staff reporters, specialist correspondents, photographers, feature writers and editors, the same as a national newspaper. It also has a radio service.

News stories appear on the screen under 'slugs' or short headings, with the time they were written or the embargo on their use, and are supplied direct to newsrooms, businesses and Parliament. Posh London clubs used to have a machine printing off the latest news from PA (supplied via a telex onto sheets of paper which were pinned up on a board) including everything from the latest Stock Exchange information to the score at the Oval. Subscribers to PA can use the material in their own publications – either wholesale, or as the basis for their own reporting of the story. PA supplies photos, diary dates and quotes online. PA also receives a blizzard of news releases on a minute-by-minute basis, and has a healthy disregard for most of them.

If a story, quote or event appears on PA, it appears in the newsrooms of virtually every important media outlet in the country. This means that a single phone call to PA can lead to coverage in dozens of newspapers, national and regional, and further coverage by the broadcasters.

HOW TO REACH THE RIGHT AUDIENCE

A solid grasp of the age, social class and particular interests of the readership of different publications will help you tailor your news story or comment accordingly and provide a better chance of your story being picked up.

There are lazy stereotypes attached to certain media outlets, for example *Guardian* readers as public sector managers with mortgages, interested in the arts and liberal causes. Or *Sun* readers as white-van-driving Conservative-voting self-employed men in the building trade. Or *Daily Mail* readers as obsessed with house prices and immigrants.

These stereotypes can be misleading. *The Sun*'s readership, both in print and online editions, is over 4.7 million, with a social class breakdown of about three million in social class C2DE and 1.7 million in social class ABC1. That means there are significantly more ABC1s (lawyers, doctors, managers, professionals) reading *The Sun* than there are reading *The Times* or *Telegraph*.

The male/female divide is split relatively evenly across most of the major newspapers in the UK. The *Daily Telegraph* (51 per cent/ 49 per cent), *The Guardian* (52 per cent/48 per cent) and the *Daily Mirror* (53 per cent/47 per cent) are all read by marginally more men than women (Media Briefing UK, 2014).

In the case of *The Sun*, this disparity increases with 58 per cent of the readership being men compared to 42 per cent women. The *Daily Star* and the *Financial Times* have a much larger difference in the proportion of men and women reading their paper, with 65 per cent men to 35 per cent women and 61 per cent men to 39 per cent women respectively (Media Briefing UK, 2014).

Perhaps the most important indicator of whether a newspaper is likely to publish your story is the social class of its readership. Our newspapers reflect the class system. The broadsheets attract a majority of readers belonging to social grade ABC1; The Guardian takes 89 per cent of its readership from here (14 per cent of these come from the highest income group A) (The Guardian, 2015) and 86 per cent of Daily Telegraph readers come from the ABC1 group (Daily Telegraph, 2015).

Tabloid readership is mainly composed of those from the C2DE social group. Sixty-four per cent of Sun readers belong to this class, along with 64 per cent of Daily Star readers and 56 per cent of readers of the Daily Mirror (Newsworks, 2016).

The UK's main mid-market newspaper, the Daily Mail, has a majority of readers from the ABC1 social grade. However, at 65 per cent, this proportion is much smaller than that of The Guardian or the Telegraph (Newsworks, 2016).

The demographic composition is important for the communications professional to know, as it will give clues about where press releases or articles are likely to be well-received, and how they can be tailored to fit in with the publication's wider message.

For example, the Daily Mirror reported research compiled by the bank Santander which showed 30 per cent of people didn't properly read or understand their bills. The article also featured some 'top tips' of how to save money on bills, such as bundling TV and broadband packages to get a better deal.

Presumably, Santander sent the news release knowing that with 56 per cent of *Daily Mirror* readers belonging to the skilled and unskilled manual worker classes, their readership was more likely to struggle to make ends meet. The story would make it into the newspaper because it appealed to the readership.

WHAT ARE JOURNALISTS LIKE?

The media is people. People reporting, presenting, producing, editing, designing, writing, rewriting, asking questions and waking up tomorrow and doing it all over again. Many of the jobs are new, such as online content editor, but the skills are old. Many of the old jobs have gone, such as 'compositing' which employed an army of people arranging letters to be printed on the page, and the apprenticeship for the job lasted seven years.

Most journalists are hard-working, committed and intelligent. Journalists tend to have a sense of professionalism and pride in their job, which they see as an essential part of the democratic process. 'Freedom of the press' as the mark of a free society is a concept they take seriously. Their belief in seeking out the truth is mostly sincere. They are serious people doing a serious job. When some of their number behave in immoral or disreputable ways of the kind exposed by the phone-hacking scandal, the majority of journalists are rightly appalled.

Journalists tend to be sceptics, querulous, interested in how things work and in people.

If you meet a journalist socially, they will ask lots of questions and after the conversation you will discover that they know a lot about you, but you don't know anything about them.

Most journalists have undergone specialist training. In the UK, journalism training is governed by the National Council for the Training of Journalists (NCTJ). The NCTJ accredits journalism qualifications in colleges and universities and maintains standards. An NCTJ qualification is a pre-requisite for most jobs in journalism (with the exception of newspaper or magazine columnists like Katie Hopkins, who require only a lively and controversial take on life.)

Many journalists have survived at the lower reaches of the profession on abysmal pay and conditions. The *Guardian Media Guide* describes the paths into the job as 'many and vague, usually mundane, and always badly paid'. Journalism is a trade where 'paying your dues' counts.

The same is not true of the new wave of 'online journalism'. The rise of the internet allows anyone to call themselves a journalist, to write articles without due regard to probity or ethics, and to publish with few of the legal safeguards under which the 'mainstream media' works.

This explosion of websites and blogs has created 'citizen journalism', which can be defined as ordinary citizens reporting and commentating on events and people, often beyond the reach of the established media organisations.

American writer Courtney Radsch defines citizen journalism as

> an alternative and activist form of newsgathering and reporting that functions outside mainstream media institutions, often as a response to shortcomings in the professional journalistic field, that uses similar journalistic practices but is driven by different objectives and ideals and relies on alternative sources of legitimacy than traditional or mainstream journalism.

This can be fantastic: providing testimony and reportage from the front line of events, such as the Arab Spring or protests in China. Or it can be terrible, badly written nonsense.

A small but significant example: someone on Twitter called Aaron Bastani claims to 'write, think and talk about technology and politics' and has 12,000 followers. In January 2016, Bastani tweeted that the recently sacked Labour shadow minister Michael Dugher had been a Conservative candidate in the 2001 general election. This is untrue. Dugher was the Labour candidate.

Yet this 'writer and thinker' tweeted it, and many thousands read it, and some people will have believed it, and not have seen the retraction and apology. On a newspaper, a political journalist would firstly have known the facts, and secondly, a sub would have checked such an incredible claim before it was published. Yet on Twitter, people can write nonsense about other people, and some of it sticks. Far from unearthing and revealing truth, social media can in reality invent and reinforce lies far more effectively than some 'MSM conspiracy'.

Despite the challenge from citizen journalism and the decline of Fleet Street and the mighty regional newspapers, journalists are still with us. They may no longer have hats affixed with a card marked 'press'. They are more likely to be offered professional support if they drink too much at lunchtime, rather than lauded for their ability to deliver 800 words after seven pints. They can no longer claim expenses which outweigh their salaries and contain claims for fine food, wine, taxis and, in the case of one Victorian journalist, hire of a horse, servant and pistol.

But the modern journalist will continue to seek out great stories which make the reader or viewer go 'wow', which expose wrong-doing and hypocrisy, and which shape our views and opinions. So spin doctors need to know with whom they are dealing.

DIFFERENT TYPES OF JOURNALIST

'Journalist' covers a variety of different job descriptions on newspapers, magazines, radio and television. The emergence of 'citizen journalism' allows just about anyone with access to the internet to call themselves a journalist.

A journalist, for our purposes, is someone involved in the writing and production of news and features for newspapers, magazines, websites, or for broadcast on radio and television. They may be working full time for a publication or broadcaster, or for an agency, or freelance. They will usually, but not always, hold an NCTJ qualification, and most likely be a member of the National Union of Journalists (NUJ).

They are central to our story because without their good-will and collaboration, your message is not going to appear in the media, and is not going to reach the people you want it to. Here are some of the main types:

Reporter

At the front line is the reporter, responsible for writing news stories, or delivering reports directly on radio or TV. On a local paper there might be only a handful; on a national newspaper, hundreds. This is the type of journalist most people feel they understand the best: the fearless crusader for truth, the tire-less scribe, the exposer of injustice, the person in your front garden if you win the lottery.

Reporters are tenacious, insatiable and querulous. They often cover a 'patch' and little takes place on it without their knowledge. They are as at home interviewing the winner of the biggest marrow competition as a visiting Cabinet minister.

Margaret Thatcher's spin doctor Bernard Ingham started out as a reporter on the *Yorkshire Post*. In 1986, Ingham ex-pressed his empathy with journalists (rather like a cheetah expressing empathy with the gazelle): 'I feel for the reporter ... I have shared with him his perishing funerals, his sodden agricultural shows, his grisly murders, his eerie ghost hunts, his endless doorsteps.'

On a national newspaper, reporters will perform astonishing feats of endurance and persistence to get the story, including staking out people's homes for days on end, blagging their way into places they shouldn't be, and offering money for stories. The 'suitcase of cash' approach is a real thing.

When people have any kind of direct contact with journalists, it is the reporter they usually face. The reporter is part of a team, and will often be given a clear steer by the news desk about how to pursue a particular story. That means they will find the angles to support the story they want.

Reporters have been immortalised in fiction, from Lois Lane and Clark Kent on the *Daily Planet*, to Damien Day, the unscrupulous TV news reporter in *Drop the Dead Donkey*, to Zoe Barnes in the US version of *House of Cards*.

Most newspaper groups run training schemes for their reporters, and a newly recruited young reporter is called a 'cub reporter'.

Specialist correspondent

A specialist correspondent is a journalist covering a particular area such as health, sport, personal finance, cooking or defence. They have job titles like 'Health Correspondent' or 'Sports Editor', and are often recognised authorities in their area of expertise.

According to the NUJ 'the specialist journalist is becoming an endangered species as short-sighted news managements cut their posts'. As Michelle Stanistreet, the general secretary of the NUJ, wrote in *The Guardian* in November 2015:

> Why do government spin doctors swerve past specialist reporters when trying to get publicity for a new policy? And why do special correspondents have a reputation with colleagues for killing stories?
>
> That's because they can tell at a glance the policy story is a piece of re-heated rubbish that eager special advisers have flogged to death, and will use their expert knowledge to pull it apart.
>
> Specialist journalists have an important role to play. They bring knowledge to a story and provide context and analysis. They will have a range of contacts they can depend on to provide informed comment. More importantly, they bring in exclusive stories.

The role reflects the changes in society. It is not that long since every paper had a couple of 'industrial correspondents' and the FT had five. Today, only the Press Association has one. There are still quite a few 'royal correspondents' and 'celebrity and show business' correspondents.

They almost certainly know more about their subject than you do. What they need is high levels of detail and insight. They want stories which are about the inside machinations of institutions, about policy developments, and about the personalities in a particular sector. They don't need general news.

Some examples are Fergus Walsh, the medical correspondent for the BBC, and Jeff Powell, boxing correspondent for the *Daily Mail*.

News editor

This is a more senior position, responsible for allocating stories to reporters, deciding priorities and angles and usually reporting to the editor. The news editor is usually a journalist with a few more years' experience, but who has often been promoted through the ranks of news reporters.

Sub-editor

This is a specialist function. The sub-editors ('subs') receive the reporters' articles ('copy') via the newspaper's computer system, and 'weave their magic' (if you believe the subs) or 'hack it to pieces' (if you believe the reporters). The subs' job is to check spelling, grammar, house style and length of the piece, all of which they might change.

They write captions for photographs, 'panels' (the sections of text pulled out of an article and placed between two lines, used to break up long articles) and 'standfirsts' (the text between the headline and the main text, often used on features and longer news pieces.) The subs also layout the page.

Subbing might be extremely heavy, in the case of a tabloid newspaper where space is at a premium, or lighter on a weekly title. Subs might phone the reporter for clarification, or refer the article to the lawyers for legal checking.

Subs are also the heroes of the headline. On the tabloids, where daring, attention-grabbing headlines are the most important part of the paper, the subs' craft can be best seen.

The sub does not write the story, which is why you can often observe a disconnect between the content of a news story, or an opinion piece by a columnist, and the headline. The headline says one thing, but if you read the story it doesn't quite match. That's why there's no point complaining to reporters about headlines, because they're not responsible for them.

Editor

On a newspaper, the editor is the boss with whom the buck stops. They will be a journalist of many years' standing, and seek to influence the overall style, content and tone of the paper. Usually the editor will report directly to the owner of the paper. On national newspapers, the job title 'editor' covers the larger-than-life characters of Fleet Street legend. Famous Fleet Street editors down the decades have included Rebekah Brooks, Dominic Lawson, William Rees-Mogg, Kelvin MacKenzie, Andy Coulson, Paul Dacre, Harold Evans, Piers Morgan, Charles Wintour and Eve Pollard.

Contemporary newspaper and magazine editors include:

- John Witherow: *Times*
- Katharine Viner: *Guardian*
- Lionel Barber: *Financial Times*
- Chris Evans: *Daily Telegraph*
- Lloyd Embley: *Mirror*
- Tony Gallagher: *Sun*
- Paul Dacre: *Daily Mail*

- Hugh Whittow: *Express*
- Zanny Minton Beddoes: *Economist*
- Fraser Nelson: *Spectator*
- Sarah Sands: *Evening Standard*

In TV and radio, the editor is in overall charge of a particular programme or series, in the same way as a newspaper editor, just without the glamour. For example, the editor of *Newsnight* is Ian Katz, and the editor of the *Today* programme is Jamie Angus. They are responsible for the overall tone and content, and take the rap if something goes wrong or provokes complaints.

Section editor

On a newspaper, different parts of the paper will have separate editors, for example the business pages editor, the women's pages editor, or the colour supplement editor.

Producer

In radio and TV, the producer is responsible for the technical production of a programme or section of a programme (a 'package').

Assistant producer (AP)

In radio and TV, this is a more junior version of the producer, working to a producer, and often learning on the job. This role should not be confused with production assistant (PA), who is the person (often young and female) responsible for the administrative side of programme-making such as booking cars for guests, sorting out locations, expenses and ordering the sandwiches.

Researcher

These are the people in TV, usually young and thrusting, who provide the ideas, planning and research for programmes. They are the people who will read news releases, monitor the newspapers and rival stations, spot trends and come up with imaginative ideas. They tend to be starting out in the business, and want to be promoted to APs or reporters. For spin doctors, they can be a useful first contact to collaborate on the incubation of a story, long before it appears.

Freelances

Freelances are journalists who sell their services to different news organisations, but are not directly employed. It is an extremely tough way to make a living. Freelances live a life of feast or famine, at times chasing down stories and churning out copy, and at other times staring at an empty fridge and crying. The most important tools for a freelance journalist are an insatiable curiosity married to an adaptable writing style, plus a good accountant. Spin doctors tend to view freelances with some suspicion because they can be hard work, without the promise of a story actually appearing.

Columnists and bloggers

One of the results of the digital revolution is the growth in 'comment' rather than news. Columnists and bloggers offer up 800 words on their take on the world of politics, sport, entertainment or whatever. As Harry Evans once said: 'In journalism it is simpler to sound off than it is to find out.'

Some columnists are specialists, with inside tracks into their specialist fields, for example political columnists such as Matthew d'Ancona, Matthew Parris, Steve Richards or Polly Toynbee. For the political spin doctors, these guys are incredibly important, because of the influence they have in shaping public debate, in introducing new policy ideas, and in commentating on individuals' performances and prospects.

Others are entertaining, lively writers giving us their views on contemporary culture and life, such as Caitlin Moran.

Not to be confused with sketch writers such as Ann Treneman or Quentin Letts, who write pithy, acerbic, often scurrilous accounts of debates in Parliament or other serious events.

Chapter Four

Dealing with Journalists

Spinning a story involves twisting it to one's advantage, using surrogates, press releases, radio actualities, and other friendly sources to deliver the line from an angle that puts the story in the best possible light. Successful spinning involves getting the media to 'play along', by convincing them through briefings, backgrounders, or other methods of persuasion — that a particular spin to the story is the correct one. Sometimes the spinner can accomplish the same result not by persuading reporters, but by simply making life easy for them ... briefings and press conferences serve as a watering hole for packs of journalists in search of news ... well choreographed photo-opportunities provide striking visual images that reinforce the messages that White House officials want to convey.

—JOHN ANTHONY MALTESE, SPIN CONTROL

Basically you're all overpaid and we hate you.

—Department of Trade and Industry
(DTI) press officer to a journalist

JOURNALISTS WILL DECIDE quickly whether or not you are wasting their time. Journalists want you to be fast, efficient, and above all useful in your dealings with them. They want you to help them do their job better. You can achieve this by giving them stories, secrets, ideas, information, pictures, interviews and quotes.

You can fail to do this by trying to persuade them your dull non-story is the stuff of front pages, that your news story is the most important thing to happen that day, and by failing to understand what the journalist needs and what their deadlines are. If you really want to annoy a journalist, try telling them something is or isn't news. They consider that judgement to be theirs, not yours.

Part of the skill of a journalist is being able to sniff out a time waster on the end of a phone and get rid of them, or to spot a source who may be of some use in filling that blank column on page four.

A spin doctor should be a professional, on friendly terms with journalists, and with an understanding of how things work.

Unlike, for example, the Conservative MP for Telford, Lucy Allan, who was subject to the following report in The Independent in January 2016:

Tory MP Lucy Allan pulls out of BBC interview after being told she can't veto questions

A Conservative MP has pulled out of a BBC interview after she was told she could not veto the questions she would be asked, the broadcaster has reported.

Lucy Allan, the MP for Telford, told BBC Shropshire that she wanted to be 'sure that malicious false allegations made by "aliases" were not repeated as if fact on a mainstream serious political programme'.

She later denied the accusations, posting on Twitter: 'I never asked to veto questions – this is getting pretty nasty. I wonder who made that slur up.' She added that she was 'hoping for an apology' from the broadcaster.

Good luck with that.

We'll look at the nuts and bolts of dealing with the media later on – the story development, briefings, social media, photographs and so on. Before we do, there are some basic techniques which put you in the 'useful' category.

BE AVAILABLE

The image in fiction of the spin doctor with a mobile phone permanently clamped to their ear is not far from the truth. A spin doctor has to be always available, into two directions: upwards and outwards. Upwards to their boss, and outwards to the media.

The partners and spouses of spin doctors know the horrors of interrupted holidays, funerals, weddings, school plays and dinner parties. The phone goes all the time, day and night, and the spin doctor is expected to take the call: in a restaurant, in the bath, or in bed. Not only does the spin doctor need to take the call, they need to provide the caller with something useful, and fast. An inconvenient call received can often spur a series of calls made, in search of the relevant information.

You often see the same names being quoted in newspapers and the same faces and voices on interviews. Is this because these people have special insights or knowledge which make them more worthy of interview? No, it usually means that they were the first ones to agree to the bid.

When programme makers are looking for interviewees, they may phone around four or five people to fill one slot. Whoever comes back and says yes first gets the interview. Next time, the programme might phone that person first of all. If you say yes and make yourself available at all hours of the day and night (and give good interviews), you will be asked again and again.

SPEED KILLS

Spin doctoring is about being fast. It's about dropping what you were doing, and reacting quickly. It means understanding that journalists are working to deadlines, with editors breathing down their necks. If a journalist phones you for some information or a quote, they need answers within minutes, not days. This is why Twitter is so useful, because it serves as a news wire, getting rebuttal, reaction and quotes into the public space within seconds.

Beating your spin doctoring opponent means being faster than them. The slogan 'speed kills' appeared on the wall of the Clinton War Room during the US Presidential elections in 1992. Under the direction of James Carville and George Stephanopoulos, the Clinton camp had their reaction to events so finely tuned that they could have the Clinton response and rebuttal to a George Bush Snr speech with journalists before Bush even sat down. That meant that time and time again, the news story was not what Bush had said, but what Clinton was saying about what Bush had said.

As a news story develops in the 24-hour world of online, radio and TV, the angle of the story can be altered by new information on a minute-by-minute basis. The role of social media is to turn and twist a story away from its original trajectory. A quote or picture on Twitter can change a story's dynamic, like a flock of birds suddenly changing direction as one.

The way journalists use interviews during the news cycle changes hour by hour. In a disaster situation, the first bulletins feature eye-witnesses. Later bulletins feature interviews with the emergency services. Later on, the airline whose plane has crashed, or the country where the earthquake happened will deploy spokesmen. Last to appear, on BBC Two's Newsnight and Radio 4's World Tonight, will be 'experts' on flight safety, terrorism, earthquakes, hostage psychology or food poisoning, depending on the disaster.

Spin doctors need to understand deadlines. For a huge news story, front pages can be altered and news bulletins changed at the last minute. Newspapers can change layout from edition to edition on the same day – or even produce special editions to cover a major story such as the death of a royal. News bulletins can be interrupted during broadcast with a major news story.

To influence the news agenda, you have to be ahead of the game, and that means operating well in advance of deadlines. For a daily newspaper, you should aim for late afternoon the previous day, at the very latest. For a Sunday, it should be Friday afternoon. Weekly magazines can take news three to four days in advance of publication, but will have their features worked out weeks in advance. Glossy monthlies like *Cosmopolitan* are designed months in advance. With an online publication, the deadline might be a few minutes from now.

SPOON-FEEDING

The basic job of the spin doctor is to help journalists create news, features, comment and analysis. Journalists do not have the time for interpreting complex data or reading lengthy reports, and this is a great opportunity to 'help' the journalist in their job by providing handy summaries and guidance.

The popular image of a journalist is that of a news-hound with a notepad in their hand, but the reality is that most journalists are desk-bound, filtering an enormous amount of material that comes to them from the television, radio, news wires, emails and telephones.

Harold Evans writes in his *Essential English*: 'Enough news is arriving today at any large newspaper office to make four or five fat novels and fill the news columns many times over.'

Modern journalism is as much about filtering, sorting, prioritising and editing as it is about finding things out. A charitable view of journalists may be that they spend their time chasing leads, checking sources and ferreting out the truth, but with a deadline looming and pressure to find a story, none is averse to a little spoon-feeding from spin doctors.

Damian McBride, in his memoir *Power Trip*, which gives an account of his time as a spin doctor, describes writing whole paragraphs for journalists to drop into their articles, quotes from his boss Gordon Brown, and even an entire interview, complete with questions and answers, when Brown's famous temper had ruined a real interview conducted at the back of an aeroplane on the return from a summit.

WHO'S TALKING?

You need to be really clear on what basis you're dealing with journalists. In politics, conversations within the walls of the Palace of Westminster are considered to be on 'lobby terms'. If a politician tells a journalist something on 'lobby terms' it means that they can report it but they can't say who gave them the information. This covers a great deal of subterfuge and briefing.

In the wider world of journalism, you need to be clear on what basis you're giving information to a journalist.

There is a broadly understood formula for speaking to journalists, but you should clarify beforehand if you've never dealt with the journalist before. If you don't, everything and anything you say will be considered 'on the record' and reportable.

The different types of attribution are:

'On the record': all that is said can be quoted and attributed.

'Unattributable': what is said can be reported but not attributed.

'Off the record': the information is provided to inform a decision or provide a confidential explanation, not for publication.

'On background': the information in the briefing can be used, but no direct quotes or attribution.

'On deep background': the same as above, but the journalist will do their best to obscure the source of the briefing.

There is some confusion about the exact meaning of these terms, and therefore a danger of them being misinterpreted. In *Power Trip*, Damian McBride recounts how he would challenge unauthorised briefers:

> If I ever caught a colleague who wasn't supposed to speak to the press
> having a chinwag with a hack, I wouldn't ask them what they'd been
> saying, I'd ask: 'What terms were you speaking on?'
>
> 'What?' they'd invariably reply, at least the first time.
>
> 'Well, you know. Was it in your own name or as a source? Was
> it "on the record" or "off the record"? Was it "not for use" or just
> "no fingerprints"? Was it "on background" or just "operational"?

Was it "you can't act on this" or just "you didn't get this from me"? You know, which of those?'

The best possible advice, if you're new to all this and have no long-term relationship with the journalist, is to ignore all these grades of secrecy and give the journalist nothing that you're not entirely happy to see in print. This is the 'Daily Mail test' – say and do nothing that you wouldn't mind being in the Daily Mail tomorrow.

TIMING

In dealing with the media, as in comedy, timing is everything. Because of the relentless regime of deadlines, you have to time your announcements and activities to fit into the journalists' timetables. You also have to time your activities to give yourself maximum advantage.

There are times of the year when it's easier to get stories into the newspapers – such as over the summer (the so-called 'Silly Season'), or between Christmas and New Year. This is because much of national life has shut down, and journalists are looking out for news. Often, the journalists on duty are covering for more senior colleagues who are in the south of France or Tuscany, so they may be more open to your approaches. National newspapers come out on a Monday, but often not much happens on a Sunday, so if you offer your story on a 'Sunday for Monday' you might be lucky.

If you find yourself the primary contact with the media, you must prepare yourself to work every hour of the day. Calls will come into your mobile from the very early morning as breakfast broadcasters sort out their running orders and guests, through to late at night when the first editions of newspapers appear and trigger a flurry of new news and comment, often picked up by broadcasters, and sometimes in need of correction or rebuttal.

After 1997, the Labour Party in government had a 'conference call' of politicians and their spin doctors late on a Saturday night to go through the first editions of the Sunday papers, and agree the 'lines to take' on the stories.

The worst kind of media call is from a Sunday newspaper on a Friday night or a Saturday morning, asking for reaction to some sort of scandal. You have to get your strategy sorted swiftly, at the exact time offices are emptying and senior folks are heading for the hills.

Damaging announcements can be timed to minimise their impact. Jo Moore famously sent an email suggesting releasing a government announcement on councillors' allowances on 11 September 2001. She wanted to 'bury' the bad news. She was pilloried by the media when a disgruntled civil servant leaked the email to a newspaper several weeks later. The 'bad news' she sought to bury was a rise in councillors' allowances, a story so utterly trivial compared to the events of the day. Still, there are plenty of journalists who are glad their immediate thoughts and utterances were not made public when the first plane hit the tower. This was mercifully before Twitter.

You can use other people's stories, for example the Queen's ninetieth birthday, as cover to release your own difficult stories. As the Labour Party grappled with its botched reshuffle in January 2016, David Cameron slipped out an announcement that he had suspended ministerial 'collective responsibility' over the EU referendum. Most days, this would be a huge piece of news, but that day it fell down the broadcasters' running orders as Jeremy Corbyn's reshuffle descended into farce.

The results of the deadlocked reshuffle, incidentally, were finally announced by Labour spinners around midnight, thus missing most media deadlines and annoying the journalists who'd spent two days waiting for an announcement.

At the White House, unpopular announcements are bundled together on a Friday to minimise their impact. Here's fictional *West Wing* spin doctor Josh explaining the process to his assistant:

Donna: What's 'Take Out the Trash Day'?

Josh: Friday.

Donna: I mean what is it?

Josh: Any stories we have to give the press that we're not wild about we give all in a lump on Friday.

Donna: Why do you do it in a lump?

Josh: Instead of one at a time?

Donna: I'd think you'd want to spread them out.

Josh: They've got X column inches to fill, right? They're gonna fill them no matter what.

Donna: Yes.

Josh: So if we give them one story, that story's X column inches.

Donna: And if we give them five stories...

Josh: They're a fifth the size.

Donna: Why do you do it on Friday?

Josh: Because no one reads the paper on Saturday.

Donna: You guys are real populists, aren't you?

'Take out the trash day' doesn't work so well in the digital age, when there is limitless space for stories online. That doesn't stop government spin doctors from doing it anyway. On 18 December 2015, just as Parliament was closing for Christmas, the government made thirty-six written ministerial statements and issued 424 government documents.

These included reports on unnecessary deaths in the NHS, on the cost of ministerial chauffeurs, an increase in the number of special advisers, the salary details of the highest-paid public officials, and the news that the government had lost track of 10,000 asylum seekers.

If you didn't notice, you were probably at a Christmas party.

NO 'NO COMMENT'

Old movies sometimes depict characters besieged by reporters saying 'no comment' as they rush past them. Saying 'no comment' is the act of someone who watches too much television. It is as removed from the real world of news as journalists with a label marked 'press' sticking out of the band in their hats, and people in newsrooms shouting 'hold the front page'.

There no such thing as 'no comment'. 'No comment' is a comment.

To a journalist, 'no comment' means 'the only comment I have to make is that I am guilty of something, have something to hide, or am engaged in a major cover-up, so you had better chase this story like your life depends on it'.

There can also be dangers in issuing straightforward denials, because the denial can provide a peg for the story ('So-and-so angrily denied reports last night that he was a heroin addict').

The spin doctor must be able to comment and deal with adverse publicity as well as the good stuff. The best examples of 'crisis management' are when the polluting oil company or retailer caught selling poisonous cat food has been as open and honest as possible. Open public relations and genuine contrition can turn a situation round.

BE HONEST

If you lie, you are finished. It will destroy your reputation as a professional, and sour your relationships with journalists. However, your role is not to release all of the truth, all of the time. Your skill lies in knowing how and when to release parts of the truth in ways which help. Sometimes you have to skate on thin ice.

ACCESS TO THE ORGAN GRINDER

Usually, the spin doctor is the conduit for information between the journalist and a senior figure, or the 'sewer, not the sewage', as John Biffen once said of Bernard Ingham. Often, the spin doctor acts as a lightning conductor for their boss, taking the flak and diverting criticism.

In the USA, political spin doctors can even take part in public debates and media appearances themselves, as commentators in their own right. We have yet to see that development over here, thank heavens, although ex-spin doctors such as Alastair Campbell and John McTernan can appear as pundits.

The practising spin doctor must not be a barrier, and from time to time must facilitate access to his or her boss for journalists. That means setting up briefings, lunches, news conferences, interviews and private meetings for journalists from time to time. Journalists sometimes want to hear what the organ grinder has to say, not just listen to the chattering of the monkey.

HOW TO SPOT JOURNALISTS' TRICKS

I once asked a journalist about the trickery that journalists engage in to get a story. He replied: 'There is no trickery, just good journalism.' Whatever the definition, we can agree that journalists use a range of techniques to get a story, especially if someone doesn't want them to know it, ranging from simple psychological tricks to elaborate sting operations.

A good journalist can use cajolery, flattery, bribery and threats just as effectively as a good spin doctor. It is not for nothing that journalists in American political slang are known as 'scorps' (short for scorpions). Like their deadly namesakes, scorps have plenty of sting in their tale.

Here are some of the main techniques to watch out for:

'Would you say that...'

One of the oldest tricks in the book is the ascribing of quotes to individuals on the basis of a grunt of assent or a nod of the head. It runs as follows: the journalist says 'Would you say that the redundancies your firm is making will devastate the community?' You reply 'Yes in the short term, but in the medium term our £3 million retraining package will get people back to work.' Result? Headlines screaming 'DEVASTATION: firm predicts job loss chaos.'

Be warned: anything a journalist says and you agree with, or even fail to disagree with, can be reported as your own words. The best way to avoid the 'would you say...' trap is to categorically deny the views expressed, and offer something else instead. Never repeat back the negative phrase that's been put to you. Simply refuse to accept the premise of the question.

In the original *House of Cards*, the fictional Prime Minister Francis Urquhart's way of dealing with it (if the journalist had got the right end of the stick) was to say 'You might say that, I couldn't possibly comment.'

The Pinter pause

In a normal conversation, a pause in the flow of conversation is deemed a social embarrassment, and the natural inclination for most people is to fill the silence with something, anything, usually the first thing that comes into your head.

Journalists use this natural inclination to trick people into saying more than they intended, or to stray off-message. It is important to remember that a broadcast interview, or a telephone call from a journalist, is not a normal conversation, and the usual social rules of engagement are suspended.

Lengthy Pinter-esque silences from journalists are designed to make you blabber on and hopefully give something away. You should simply repeat your points over and over again. Or you ask the journalist a question, such as 'are we done?'. Sometimes, spin doctors' conversations with journalists can contain seemingly endless pauses, with each side waiting to see who cracks first.

Wood for the trees

One trick is for the journalist to decide what information they want, and disguise their true intentions in a forest of other questions. Usually this takes the form of lengthy questions about the interviewee's area of expertise, designed to lull them into a false sense of security, and the killer question is casually thrown in towards the end. When people complain about being quoted 'out of context' this is usually what they mean.

A variation on this approach is the Columbo technique: firing the killer question when your guard is down. Columbo, the '70s detective, would act like a bumbling dolt, and then deliver the killer question which tore apart the suspect's alibi, with the preamble 'there's just one thing bothering me...'. Journalists can use same technique.

I know your boss...

This is a straightforward bluff where the journalist gives the impression they've spoken to someone higher up the food chain than you. They imply they already know the information they are after, so that the spin doctor inadvertently gives the game away. It can usually work if the hack pretends to be best mates with your boss, or your boss's boss, and to have received the information first-hand.

If in doubt, make it up...

Some journalists, in the absence of real information, simply make up quotes to back up their stories. Quotes can appear from 'sources close to...' or 'one backbencher, who said last night...' and they could be anyone; no one will ever know whether it was really said by a real person, or crafted by a harassed hack with a looming deadline.

Alastair Campbell mentioned this in a piece in the *Mirror* on 3 July 2000: 'If you read about a senior insider, the place the insider is from is likely to be the journalist's head.'

Internal criticism from within an organisation can be invented, because no one will admit to it anyway, and quotes can usually be made up to substantiate stories about football transfers, royal marriage rifts and Cabinet rows. No one will ever know for sure.

Sometimes journalists go too far and spoil it for the rest. In 2003, *New York Times* journalist Jayson Blair was exposed as a fraud for making up quotes, eye-witness accounts and even whole stories. In 2011, the journalist Johann Hari lost his job on *The Independent* and his Orwell Prize when it became apparent that he had been lifting quotes from famous people in other people's interviews and articles, and placing them in his own articles to look like the interviewee had said those things to him.

Here's how *The Guardian* reported another faker at the *New York Times*, Jack Kelley:

New 'fake stories' row hits US media

Some of the details uncovered in the investigation of Kelley's work were truly astonishing. The paper examined Kelley's claim to have been an eyewitness at a 2001 suicide bombing in Jerusalem. In his original copy Kelley had written that he saw three men have their heads blown off in the blast. In a first draft of his piece he described how the heads rolled 'with their eyes still blinking'. However, police records show that no adult victims of the blast were decapitated.

In another story Kelley visited Cuba in February 2002 and wrote a powerful piece describing a group of six refugees heading off to

America in a boat. But, he claimed, a storm sank the craft a few days later and no one survived. Kelley produced a picture of a woman among the group called Yacqueline which was used along with the story. But far from dying at sea, she was tracked by the USA Today team alive and well and living in America. Her real name was Yamilet Fernández and she had worked at a hotel in Cuba before moving to America a year ago as a legal immigrant.

So don't believe everything you read in the newspapers, because your 'news' might be fiction. As George Orwell once wrote: 'Early in life I had noticed that no event is ever correctly reported in a newspaper.'

KEY POINTS

- Your job is to supply news and views, and the media need you as much as you need them.

- Use a variety of techniques.

- Journalists have a full armoury of tricks, so watch out.

- Timing is everything.

- Sometimes journalists make stuff up.

TAKE NOTES

All of the above proves that when you are dealing with journalists you should always take notes of the conversation. A journalist will have a note of the conversation, traditionally in shorthand on a reporters' notepad, but today as likely to be a tablet or phone. Much time and effort was spent during the Hutton Inquiry looking at the records of conversations between Andrew Gilligan and Dr David Kelly held on the former's handheld computer, not a shorthand pad.

It is worth having your own version as evidence for public inquiries, court cases, or simply disputes with the editor. Bernard Ingham, when working for Margaret Thatcher, kept a flawless shorthand note of almost every conversation he had with every journalist, official and politician he encountered, giving him huge powers of recall.

CONTACT-BUILDING

Spin doctoring is a contact sport and contacts are the spin doctors' life-blood. Spinning to a journalist with whom you have an on-going relationship based on trust is much more likely to be successful than a 'cold call' to an unknown journalist. The spin doctor should nurture contacts with journalists, offer help and advice, give them occasional favours and special treatment, but always be prepared to challenge them.

Most of the time, your contact with journalists will be on

the telephone. There are not many stories in the journalist's busy day that cannot be handled with a phone call and follow-up email with extra background briefing. If your contact with the journalist is likely to be on-going, you might suggest a drink or lunch, or to meet up at a conference or event at which you will be both be present. If lunching with a journalist, it is a good idea to have some gossip or story ideas up your sleeve to make your guest feel that their time has not been wasted.

The process of holding onto and using contacts works well because journalists are trained to build their lists of useful sources of news and information, and that should include you. The spin doctor's contacts book is filled with the names of journalists, and the journalist's is filled with spin doctors.

Bill Clinton maintained card-index files in shoeboxes on every useful person he met from his college days onwards, until he became President of the United States. His biographer Martin Walker claims

> there was never a more assiduous maintainer of acquaintance and friendship than Clinton, and his political network was extraordinary... Names, addresses, phone numbers and birthdays, weddings and children, updated with new jobs and the latest publications, new meetings and family bereavements, they were all cross referenced, with a note of any campaign contributions they had made.

When the cards were finally transferred onto computer, there were more than 10,000 files.

The importance of having 'contacts' can be over-played. If your story is strong enough, and if you have something journalists want, it won't matter if you've never spoken before. Similarly, if your story is ropey, a journalist will not write it up simply because you bought them lunch. However, if a journalist needs a quote from a particular viewpoint, and there are a number of people and organisations capable of supplying the quote, the journalist will go for the one he or she knows best and can be trusted to come up with a decent, punchy quote on the spot.

The contacts book is probably the most important tool of the trade. Tales abound of panic-stricken spin doctors who have realised their little black book of contacts has been lost. These days, though, everyone is on LinkedIn or Twitter, and you can soon rebuild your contact list.

Chapter Five

In the News or In the Bin?

*Literature is the art of writing something that will be read
twice; journalism what will be grasped at once.*

—CYRIL CONNOLLY

TECHNIQUES SUCH AS the ones in the previous
chapter are never enough on their own.

You need a good story to sell. If what you're
selling is duff, no amount of spin is going to help.
You can't, in the immortal phrase, put lipstick on a pig. Or if
you do, you just end up with a nice-looking pig.

Where people often go wrong is in assuming that what's

interesting to them will be interesting to a journalist. It's not enough to be worthy, you've got to be newsworthy.

Successful journalists have an instinct for what makes a good story. They can sniff one out like a truffle-hound. There are elements which make a good story. It must contain people, emotions and novelty, and be compelling and memorable.

The first criterion is that news is only news if it is reported. On Boxing Day 2004 an earthquake in the Indian Ocean created tsunami waves which wiped out thousands of miles of coastline from Thailand to Somalia, and killed tens of thousands of people. On each of the hundreds of beaches affected by the walls of water were individual stories of heroism and tragedy: brave rescues, families destroyed, and lucky escapes.

In only a handful of cases were these stories told through the media. This doesn't make the untold stories any less heroic or tragic. But without a journalist there to report the events, there is no story. This is particularly true in television news: no pictures, no story.

On any day of the year, the newspapers and broadcasters have more news than the space or time available. Choices must be made and judgements applied. Reporters decide which two or three stories to focus their efforts on, and editors decide which ten or twenty stories will ultimately appear.

Even if a reporter has written a story, the editor may choose not to let it appear. In the days of hot metal, the paper bearing the story would have been placed on a metal spike – hence the expression 'spiked', meaning dropped or unused. This might be a story that you, as the spin doctor, have worked on for months. It might be dropped at the last minute, or mightily diminished, because Kim Kardashian has chipped a fingernail.

WHAT MAKES THE NEWS?

One view of 'what is news' is offered by the international news agency Reuters: 'Fires, explosions, floods ... railway accidents, destructive storms, earthquakes, shipwrecks ... accidents ... street riots ... strikes ... the suicide of persons of note, social or political, and murders of a sensational or atrocious character.' That was issued by Reuters in 1883.

Organisations run on budgets, reports, committee decisions, strategies and targets – but journalism is about people. Harold Evans, former *Times* and *Sunday Times* editor, said: 'News is people. It is people talking and people doing.' Editor of the *Daily Express* Arthur Christiansen advised his staff: 'Always always always tell the story through people.'

So a spin doctor has to turn the dry dust of budgets, reports and committee decisions into stories about people – who's happy, who's sad, who's up, and who's down? What do people think and feel? What are they saying and doing?

When a story can be illustrated with 'case studies', testimony from what politicians patronisingly call 'real people', or great pictures, it stands greater chance of success.

How can the spin doctor persuade a journalist that their story is news? An analysis of news stories in print and broadcast can help us understand the types of stories which appear.

Say you want to get a story into the *Liverpool Echo*. You need to read the *Liverpool Echo*, observe the kinds of stories which appear day in, day out, in the print edition and online, make a note of the names of the journalists writing news stories, and try to create a story which 'fits' with the *Echo*'s editorial decisions.

By understanding the media we are targeting we can mould the information we have into a form which a journalist will recognise and find interesting.

If you start from the premise that your story is worthy and interesting, and a journalist should be motivated by the same things you are, you are probably going to fail.

This is hard for organisations and institutions which believe what they are doing is interesting to others. Inside an organisation, the role of the spin doctor is often to battle internal attitudes about what the organisation should be telling the outside world. Often, the spin doctor brings the mindset of the journalist into the organisation, as well as taking the organisation's message out to the media.

The trick to dealing with the media is to craft your stories into formats and styles which match your target media as closely as possible.

One useful test to apply to your stories is the 'Hey Doris' test, used by *Sun* journalist Wendy Henry during the '80s, when the Currant Bun was edited by Kelvin MacKenzie. Unless a story might provoke a *Sun* reader to exclaim to her friend: 'Hey Doris, take a look at this...' the story didn't make it into the paper.

HOW TO APPLY THE 'SO WHAT?' TEST

For most stories we might offer journalists we should be aiming to the pass the 'so what?' test. Journalists, like the rest of us, have a broad understanding of what organisations do and how the world works. If your story contains nothing more interesting than 'charity raises funds', 'politician makes speech', 'business holds sale', 'public services provide services to the public' or 'football team plays football', then don't be disappointed if the reaction to your story is 'so what?'.

Local newspapers often fall foul of the 'so what?' test, as this piece from the *Mid-Sussex Times* in 2012 shows:

> **Early shoppers at Boots in South Road, Haywards Heath, found the store closed this morning.**
>
> A sign on the door said: 'Due to unforeseen circumstances we do not have a pharmacist at present and so are unable to open this store.
>
> 'The store will open as soon as a locum pharmacist arrives, unfortunately we don't yet know what time this will be.
>
> 'We apologise for any inconvenience caused and thank our customers for their patience.' The store later opened.

A surprising number of news stories pitched to journalists, brimming with news of 'groundbreaking developments' in tractor technology or the latest thoughts of a middle manager in the frozen dessert business to the 'Puddings 2020' conference in Harrogate, fail this simple test.

As we shall see, part of the spin doctor's art is taking the mundane and commonplace and turning it into something unusual and newsworthy. It's also worth saying that the process is desperately unfair. A story may fly one day, but be bounced down the agenda on another. You might plan for weeks, and see your story vanish as a major celebrity dies or some other major global news breaks.

You may find a story cooked up in a matter of moments outshines some piece of research that a team has worked on for months. Or you may get lucky, and some piece of nonsense hits the headlines because it's a slow news day.

NEWS VALUES

At the heart of any compelling news story is one or more of the following news values. News values are what make a story newsworthy. Journalists are taught news values at college, but once they start work and the relentless tyranny of the deadline takes over, they become instinctive. If you boil down every story in today's newspapers and broadcasts, they will contain one or more of these 'news values'.

Novelty

'Novelty' comes from the adjective 'novus' which translates as 'new' or 'young' or 'fresh'. News stories have to contain news – something which we are reading or hearing for the first time. There is a famous journalism adage that: 'Dog bites

man, that's not news. But man bites dog – now *that's* news.'
That means for a story to be newsworthy it should contain
something surprising, counter-intuitive and challenging.
If a dog bites a man, we would think 'so what? Dogs bite men
all the time.' But if a man bites a dog, we want to know why.
We want to know who the man was, where it happened,
why he did it and how he felt afterwards.

This story from the *Daily Telegraph* (6 January 2016) is
pure 'man bites dog', and great news for fans of a full English breakfast.

Black pudding hailed as a 'superfood'
Loaded with protein, potassium, calcium, and magnesium, as well
as being virtually carb-free, it is expected to fly off the shelves.

This from *The Independent* (8 January 2016) documented the
destruction of a giant statue in China, where we're more used
to seeing leaders revered at every opportunity.

**Mao statue in China pulled down after 120ft gold giant
is mocked online**
The Chinese authorities appear to have destroyed a giant gold
statue of Mao Zedong after it became the subject of online mockery
around the world.

Oddity

Something can be new without being odd. But oddity gives

us a new dimension. In the tabloids, this can stray into the lurid, shocking, weird or just plain sickening.

From the *Daily Mirror*, 8 January 2016:

Adolf Hitler 'faked his death then fled to Tenerife' CIA veteran claims
A veteran CIA agent claims to have proof Hitler faked his own death in his bunker at the end of the Second World War. The team have never-before-seen documents to develop the theory he did not actually kill himself and instead fled to the Canary Islands.

The *Evening Standard* (25 September 2015) highlighted that there's such a thing as excessive enthusiasm for a political figure:

Ukip supporter shows off her Nigel Farage tattoo at party's conference
A Ukip supporter has been showing off her Nigel Farage tattoo at the party's conference in Doncaster today.

Kerrie Webb, a branch secretary for Chesterfield, smiled as she was photographed displaying the inking of the Ukip leader's face on her right arm.

A similar story appeared in January 2016, when eighteen-year-old Hannah Stock got a tattoo of Ed Miliband's face on her leg. Her mum refused to talk to her afterwards.

Finally, *The Guardian* (16 December 2015) highlighted what happens when the traditional political candidates have little to offer the public:

Disgruntled Siberian city wants cat for mayor

Fed up with corruption and nepotism among local officials, residents of a far-flung Siberian city are yearning for a different kind of political representation.

Barsik the cat has been propelled to stardom after finishing far ahead of his human rivals for the post of mayor of Barnaul in an unofficial poll run by a popular regional social media page.

Political apathy and resentment over corruption scandals at city hall helped the 18-month-old Scottish Fold claw nearly 91 per cent of more than 5,400 votes cast by Tuesday.

Conflict

All kinds of stories are written up as conflicts: politics, sport, business, celebrities and campaigns. There is little room in journalism for nuance or subtlety – stories are often conflated into one side bashing the hell out of another. Two celebrities having a row on Twitter; a beleaguered football manager being booed by the club's fans; Cabinet ministers tussling over policy; London's cabbies protesting about Uber; a community campaign against a new block of yuppie flats: these are the kinds of conflicts that make a good story.

How about this, regarding the infamous Labour permareshuffle of January 2016. News stories about the resignation of Cat McKinnell MP were keen to highlight her disagreements with her leader Jeremy Corbyn. Yet her concerns about finding a work–life balance, which were the first issue she raised in her resignation letter, were largely ignored.

This is from the Huffington Post:

Shadow Attorney General Catherine McKinnell Quits Jeremy Corbyn's Shadow Cabinet

Jeremy Corbyn's reshuffle entered its second week on Monday, after Shadow Attorney General Catherine McKinnell announced she was quitting the Labour front bench.

In her letter of resignation to the Labour leader, McKinnell said she was quitting, in part, due to the 'increasingly negative' direction the party was taking under his leadership.

Stories regarding the expected split in the Cabinet on the issue of the EU referendum were reported as a mutiny against David Cameron, like this one in the *Sunday Times* (10 January 2016):

Ministers rebel at Brexit muzzle as Cameron pushes for summer vote

David Cameron could hold an in–out referendum this summer, if he can get a deal from European counterparts, as he faces a fresh cabinet mutiny at home.

Ministers are threatening to walk out after he prevented Eurosceptic ministers from expressing their views while leaving pro-Europeans to make the case publicly for Britain to remain in the European Union.

The prime minister narrowly averted the resignation of two Cabinet ministers last week after agreeing that they could campaign for 'Brexit' without leaving the government – but only after he has secured a new deal with Brussels, expected next month.

Journalists on local papers like campaigns led by local residents, parents, businesses, especially if the target is the town hall or the government. We like to read about David versus Goliath, and side naturally with David. Here's the *Lancashire Evening Post* on controversies regarding fracking taking place in the county (27 November 2015):

> **Fracking decision 'a slap in the face to local democracy'**
> Anti-fracking protesters have reacted with horror after the government announced it would make the final decision over whether fracking will be allowed in Lancashire.
>
> Energy firm Cuadrilla is appealing against councillors' decision to refuse its bids to drill and test frack at sites at Little Plumpton near Blackpool and Roseacre, near Elswick.
>
> A public inquiry will still take place next year.

If you can build elements of conflict into your story – with challenges, demands, criticisms or protests against your opponents – it has a greater chance of being picked up by a journalist.

Scandal

We all love watching the rich and powerful come a cropper, and a good scandal can keep journalists busy for weeks. Scandals come in two basic forms: financial (people stealing money or things from other people) and sexual (people doing things with other people they shouldn't be doing). Sometimes there are drugs involved too.

For example, on Sunday 17 November 2013, the *Mail on Sunday* splashed with a story about a non-executive director of the Co-operative Bank called Paul Flowers, filmed counting wads of cash and talking about cocaine and methamphetamine. This exposé came weeks after a stumbling performance at the Treasury select committee at which he didn't seem very sure of the basic numbers surrounding the Co-op Bank's disastrous finances. Later, more lurid details appeared about rent boys, plus a connection to the Labour Party. And it turned out he was a Reverend in the Methodist Church. This created the magic combination of sex, politics, drugs, money and religion, which journalists wake up each morning and pray for.

Some newspapers specialise in scandals and have teams of reporters armed with open cheque books looking for next week's front-page victim. What makes a scandal story more potent is the lengths the victim goes to protect their reputation. If they lie or stonewall it usually ends up being worse for them.

A great irony of the John Major years is that while all around him the sky was dark with a flurry of ministers' resignation letters, his own affair with Edwina Currie remained a secret until a decade later. Even then it was not revealed by a journalist but by Edwina Currie publishing it in her diary.

Perhaps the most memorable scandal covered in the news in recent times is the MPs' expenses scandal in the *Daily Telegraph* in 2008. The exposure of this information led to the resignation of the Speaker, Michael Martin, and several MPs losing their seats, and some ending up in jail. The government's handling was slow off the mark and uncoordinated, and lacked a central strategy. As the story twisted and turned, the media, and in particular the *Daily Telegraph* team, never lost the upper hand. Politicians, on the other hand, both individually and collectively, got battered.

What newspapers consider a scandal may not always strike a chord with the reader. When businessmen, footballers or politicians are caught doing something questionable, many of us just shrug our shoulders and say 'so what?'

On other occasions, you wonder what on earth they were thinking. If you were advising someone running for a parliamentary seat, would you steer them away from dressing as the accused of one of the most controversial court cases of the year, Oscar Pistorius?

Tory candidate under fire after dressing up as Oscar Pistorius – complete with gun and fake blood

A Conservative candidate's Oscar Pistorius fancy dress costume – which included a gun and fake blood – has been branded 'stomach churning' by Labour rivals.

Gregg Peers, who is standing for the Tories in a Cumbria County by-election, was pictured on his Facebook page wearing a blood-stained South Africa yellow vest with 'PISTORIUS' written on the front and holding a toy gun.

Often what a newspaper considers a scandal reflects the paper's own editorial position on an issue. Here's *The Sun* on the 'Moet Medics' participating in January 2016's junior doctors' strike:

Moet medics: High life of docs' leaders who are heading up NHS strike

Junior doctors leading Tuesday's NHS strike over new contracts are champagne-swilling socialists.

The union reps have enjoyed lavish holidays and parties and some own £500,000 homes.

Up to 45,000 will walk out on Tuesday after the British Medical Association (BMA) failed to reach agreement with the government.

And Health Secretary Jeremy Hunt last night warned doctors a strike will harm patients and force casualty wards to close.

Here's *The Guardian* on George Osborne having an 'image adviser' (17 December 2015):

Osborne gives political adviser 42% rise amid public sector pay freeze

George Osborne has given the adviser responsible for his new image a promotion and a pay rise of more than 40%, and boosted the number of his political aides by three while asking public-sector workers to accept a pay freeze.

Thea Rogers, a close associate of Osborne, received the biggest rise among all the political special advisers across government, an increase of 42% since the figures were released last November, giving her £98,000. She is now his chief of staff.

Is it a real scandal for a top government adviser to receive such a large salary? It depends where the reader draws the line.

Tragedy (and triumph over tragedy)

Tragedies get reported, from major events like earthquakes, fires, hijackings, bomb blasts and sinking ships, to individual tales of tragedy like freak accidents, murder, cancer, drowning and car crashes. Some editions of newspapers are packed with trage-dies to the point where you wonder if it's safe to leave the house.

This is from *The Guardian* (3 September 2015):

**Will the image of a lifeless boy on a beach change
the refugee debate?**
Most of Thursday's UK national newspaper front pages were dominated by pictures of a policeman lifting the lifeless body of a three-year-old boy who had been washed up on the Turkish shore.

Similar pictures were shown on UK television news bulletins the night before. It also appeared on other global TV outlets and in many papers across Europe, in Turkey, and in many Middle East countries.

According to Turkish media, the boy was Aylan Kurdi, from Kob-ani in northern Syria, and was said to have died with his five-year-old brother. They were among 12 Syrians who drowned while attempt-ing to reach the Greek island of Kos.

Here's the *Daily Mail* (7 December 2015):

**The chaos after the storm: Thousands of devastated families
face eight months away from their homes after they were ruined
by flooding**
Thousands of families are this evening facing the 'soul-destroying'

prospect of eight months away from their homes as insurers prepare for payouts of £500 million in the aftermath of Storm Desmond.

It came as the devastating weather pattern claimed its second victim with Cumbria Police confirming that a body had been found in a search of the River Kent in Kendal after an elderly man fell into the water yesterday.

Almost 5,000 homes are still without power, while transport networks, schools and hospitals in the north of England face continued disruption.

To compound the misery, forecasters say another seven inches of rain is expected to fall across Northern Ireland, Scotland and parts of northern England between now and Thursday.

A journalistic twist on straightforward human misery is the triumph-over-tragedy story (or ToT for short). This is often a heart-warming tale of human sacrifice and courage which might serve to persuade you there's hope for the human race after all. For example, this is from the *Irish Times* (8 September 2015) as a follow-up story to a picture that went viral:

Man photographed crying with family on Kos reaches Berlin

A Syrian father who was photographed in tears as he clutched his children as they arrived at a Greek island three weeks ago has reached Berlin, according to a German tabloid.

The photograph, taken on August 16th on Kos, showed Laith Majid crying as he held his seven-year-old daughter Nour in one arm and hugging his son Taha (9) with the other, as they emerged off a flimsy boat that had taken them from Turkey.

Bild now says the family, including Majid's wife Neda and two other sons Mustafa and Ahmed, are now being accommodated in an old barracks in Spandau, in the western part of the German capital.

Or this story featured in the Huffington Post following the ISIS-inspired terrorist attacks on Paris in November 2015:

Paris attacks: Man reads touching letter to Isis fighters who killed his wife

A heart-broken husband has penned a letter to the gunmen who shot and killed the 'love of my life' in last week's Paris attacks, vowing to raise their 17-month-old son 'happy and free'.

Antoine Leiris, whose wife Helene Muyal-Leiris was among 89 people killed in the Bataclan rampage on Friday, released a touching tribute on social media.

He told Isis fighters, who tore through the French capital and killed 129 in their wake, 'I won't give you the gift of my hatred' in the two-minute audio clip.

Finally, this story from the Daily Express (5 October 2015):

Alton Towers amputee hits the catwalk with a smile as she continues inspirational recovery

Vicky Balch, 20, had her right leg amputated above the knee after being involved in the Smiler accident back in June.

The former dance student, from Leyland, Lancashire, has displayed amazing resolve in her rehabilitation.

She made her way down the runway on sparkly crutches as part of a show organised by Models of Diversity.

The fearless student showed off a stunning black strapless evening dress to incredible applause.

Ambassador for Models of Diversity Sarah O'Rourke said the organisation found the 20-year-old 'really inspirational'.

Celebrity

We live in a society obsessed by celebrity. Anyone who appears on TV and in the red tops is newsworthy. It becomes a self-fulfilling act: you are famous for being famous. In recent years, so-called 'reality' television shows have created a stream of famous-for-five-minutes demi-celebs.

The addition of celebrity is like sprinkling magical newsworthiness dust over a story. That's why spin doctors seeking to advance their cause or give their message a little extra oomph can seek to tie in a celebrity.

Celebrity transforms the mundane into the magical. This story from *The Sun* (6 January 2016) is a good example of a celebrity story. Thousands of two-year-olds start nursery every September. But when a member of the royal family makes this transition, it makes it to the front page of the paper:

Prince George enjoys his first day at nursery after William and Kate drop him off
The two-year-old wore a blue quilted jacket with a brown velvet collar and a backpack.

After the Duke and Duchess of Cambridge had 'settled him' at around 10 a.m. this morning, they left.

They picked him up a few hours later, telling friends George's first day 'had gone very well'.

The nursery, which employs five members of staff, looks after around 20 children at a time.

It is housed in a converted chapel at the end of a private drive.

And the nursery costs just £5.50 an hour or £33 a day – a far cry from nurseries around Kensington Palace which can cost upwards of £18,000 a year.

Or this story in *The Times* (12 January 2016) about a couple getting engaged. Not a story? It is when the couple are Rupert Murdoch and Jerry Hall.

Rupert Murdoch and Jerry Hall announce their engagement

Rupert Murdoch, the executive chairman of News Corporation, which owns *The Times*, has announced his engagement to Jerry Hall, the actress and former supermodel, on the Births, Marriages and Deaths page of the newspaper.

News of the impending nuptials comes after a four-month romance.

Finally, the *Sun on Sunday* seemed jubilant to get the scoop on news of Cheryl Fernandez-Versini's second divorce (10 January 2016), following months of speculation:

Revealed: Cheryl Fernandez-Versini to divorce French husband as X Factor judge has had 'enough of his jealousy'

CHERYL Fernandez-Versini is to divorce for the second time, citing her French husband Jean-Bernard's 'unreasonable behaviour'.

The *Sun on Sunday* can reveal the X Factor judge is lodging divorce papers seeking to formally to end their volatile 19-month marriage. Fight For This Love singer Cheryl, 32, wants a quickie divorce from the playboy restaurateur after becoming fed up with his jealousy.

It is understood the former Girls Aloud star has been unhappy that Jean-Bernard, 35, who Cheryl and close friends call JB, didn't like her spending time with other men. And he was angered by the amount of time his wife spent with her beloved Chihuahuas Coco and Buster.

These stories are only 'news' because they concern celebrities. No celebrity, no story.

Danger

Danger in journalism comes in all shapes and sizes: health scares, killers on the loose, faulty electrical goods, factory closures, terrorist threats to the water supplies, economic downturns, carcinogenic foodstuffs, deadly new viruses and so on. Danger is a news value which is reflected in stories about dangers to the community, or to an individual. Here are some examples.

From the *Daily Express* (16 September 2015):

ANTIBIOTIC APOCALYPSE: '10million more people will DIE each year if new drugs aren't made'

Scientists predict there would be as many as 400,000 unnecessary deaths a year across Europe because of a new antibiotic 'discovery void'. Blood poisoning from sepsis is already rising in the UK because of the 'creeping catastrophe,' they said.

Bacteria are becoming resistant to our current antibiotics, which were discovered between 1910 and 1990.

Epidemics of illnesses, such as tuberculosis, E. coli, gonorrhoea, syphilis and pneumonia, which are currently treated by antibiotics could lead to multiple deaths.

And despite efforts to limit the use of antibiotics unless absolutely necessary, their use continues to rise, claim a campaigning group of experts.

The *Daily Telegraph* warned about this seemingly unthreatening household object (16 January 2016):

Why scented candles could cause cancer

With the winter winds howling at the door, the thought of battening the hatches and lighting a scented candle is understandably appealing.

But new research suggests scented candles could actually be far more harmful than previously thought, giving off potentially dangerous levels of the toxic substance formaldehyde.

A study carried out by Professor Alastair Lewis of the National Centre for Atmospheric Science at the University of York found that an ingredient commonly used to give candles their scent mutates into formaldehyde upon contact with the air.

The Times warned about the wider dangers of immigration into Europe (11 January 2016):

Migrants 'planned sex attacks' in Cologne

New Year's Eve violence, thefts and sexual assaults on women in Cologne were 'planned' and most of the offences were carried out by asylum seekers or illegal migrants, according to German police and the justice minister.

This article in the *Daily Mirror* (19 January 2016) is a great example of a story placed by a charity to promote its issues and cause, but which is published on its merits as a newsworthy story:

Dementia sufferers face 'Russian roulette' at hospitals as thousands are discharged in middle of night

Dementia sufferers are facing a 'Russian roulette' in hospitals as staff fail to provide appropriate levels of care, a new report has warned.

Elderly patients are being handcuffed to beds, discharged from hospital in the middle of the night and denied food and pain relief, the Alzheimer's Society revealed.

Finally, the *Daily Express* (9 October 2015) warns parents about the dangers of trick-or-treating:

REVEALED: The children's Halloween costumes that catch fire in SECONDS

It comes just a year after Strictly Come Dancing presenter Claudia Winkleman's eight-year-old daughter Matilda was left badly burned when her fancy dress outfit was set alight by a candle.

The star has since welcomed a crackdown on safety laws around the costumes, which are classed as toys and therefore do not have to reach the same flammability standards as clothing.

But despite ministers ordering for children's fancy dress costumes to be tested in a nationwide safety crackdown, the outfits on sale still ignite easily.

Milestones

Milestones help us make sense of a story. We can understand the point if there's a chunky number attached to it. A story about concerns regarding the effects of welfare reform on the long-term sick and disabled is illustrated with a shock statistic in the *Daily Mail* (27 August 2015):

2,600 benefit claimants die within weeks of being ruled fit for work

At least 2,600 sick and disabled people died shortly after being declared 'fit for work' by a government contractor.

Figures released by the Department for Work and Pensions show that around 100 people per month died shortly after being ruled well enough to take a job.

Anniversaries

It seems obvious, but every year contains the first, fifth, tenth, fiftieth, 100th and 200th anniversary of historical events, battles, treaties and famous people's births and deaths. Editors like anniversary stories because they can be planned for in advance, graphics departments and picture desks can scour the archives, and writers can have time to consider their angles and do their homework.

So an editor might think: what anniversaries fall in 2016? Here's a random selection:

- One year since the terrorist attack on the offices of the *Charlie Hebdo* satirical magazine and a kosher supermarket in Paris which killed seventeen people

- 100th anniversary of the Battle of the Somme

- 350th anniversary of the Great Fire of London, which swept across the city in three days, starting in a small bakery on Pudding Lane

- 400th anniversary of William Shakespeare's death

- 950th anniversary of the Battle of Hastings, which signalled the start of the Norman conquest of England.

These anniversaries provide journalists with ideas for articles, features, documentaries and interviews. The 100th anniversary of the Battle of the Somme led to articles and programmes including this in the *Daily Mirror* (19 November 2015):

All-night vigils to mark 100th anniversary of Battle of the Somme next year
All-night vigils will be held across the country to mark the centenary of the Battle of the Somme, it has been announced.

A national vigil will be held at Westminster Abbey on June 30 next year, while other overnight events will take place in Wales, Scotland and Northern Ireland to mark the 100th anniversary of the battle in which a million people were killed or wounded.

Announcing the commemorations, Culture Secretary John Whittingdale said: 'We must never forget the scale of what happened at the Somme. More died on the first day of battle than any other day of the First World War.'

Local news outlets often use anniversaries to highlight the involvement of their community in events, such as this article from the *Accrington Observer* (7 January 2016):

REVEALED: Accrington Pals at the Battle of the Somme centenary plans

With 2016 now upon us, a series of commemoration events is being planned to mark the centenary of the Accrington Pals' devastating losses in the Battle of the Somme.

The bandstand in Oakhill Park in Accrington will host the first ever 'Pals Prom' on Armed Forces Day on June 25, with a Last Night of the Proms-style performance by the East Lancashire Concert Band.

For a spin doctor, anniversaries present opportunities to piggy-back stories which you know are going to come up. Your own organisation might have its own anniversaries. This is a good example, taken from the *Islington Gazette* (12 January 2016), of Barnardo's using its 150th anniversary to boost a campaign:

Plea for more foster carers in Islington

According to the Fostering Network, about 1,150 new foster families are needed across London during 2016.

Lynn Gradwell, director of Barnardo's in London, said: 'Across London ordinary people are doing something extraordinary – opening their hearts to help children feel secure and loved.

'More foster carers are desperately needed to give these children loving and stable care, which is why we'd like to hear from people like you.

'Barnardo's celebrates its 150th anniversary this year. The charity was one of the first to place children with families and to train foster carers so they had the right skills to look after children.'

Superlatives

Journalists love the biggest, smallest, longest, and fattest. Not the second biggest, mark you. The biggest. Superlatives can lift a story from the mundane to the newsworthy. The man who collected the biggest ball of string, the dog with the longest ears, the oldest woman to give birth: these are newsworthy.

Here's one example from the *Metro* (19 January 2016):

UK's biggest family is about to get even bigger with baby number 19 on the way

Sue Radford, 40, and Noel, 45, from Lancashire, already have 18 children together, with the youngest aged only eight-months-old.

Yet despite the huge surprise, the couple are delighted that they are having another baby.

And another from the *Hertfordshire Mercury* (18 January 2016):

Hertfordshire's longest-serving police dog retires

He has spent more than a decade solving crimes up and down the region, but now the region's longest-serving police dog is stepping down.

Spaniel Brewster, who has two different coloured eyes, is the Bedfordshire, Cambridgeshire and Hertfordshire police dog unit's oldest serving drugs, cash and weapons dog.

Now 13, he arrived in 2005 from North Yorkshire, where his owners gifted him to the police after realising he was too energetic, and finished his last shift on Sunday.

News values underpin all news stories. Take a look at today's news if you're not convinced. Only by appreciating what makes news, what makes a journalist interested and how to package and present our messages do we stand a chance of success. In the news or in the bin? It's up to you.

THE X FACTOR

We've seen what makes a good story, and what attracts a journalist's attention. Yet so much of the material presented by PR firms and in-house PR teams is destined to fail. It might be that you just get unlucky: you're launching your report on housing on the morning David Bowie dies. Or it might be a busy news day, with lots of competing stories.

You might require an added sprinkle of magic. You might need to give your story a little X factor.

Sexing it up

This vile expression entered the language with reference to the government's supposed insistence that intelligence reports into Saddam Hussein's weapons of mass destruction should be stronger, clearer and more likely to scare the life out of us. It already runs the risk of becoming overused and meaningless.

What it describes, however, is a process in which spin doctors engage every day. If you're campaigning for a cause, or getting your company noticed, or plugging your client's new book or film, you have to sex it up. You have to highlight the exciting, positive, upbeat elements of your message. You have to make it sound interesting and newsworthy. If you don't sound enthusiastic, why should anyone care what you say?

The important thing here is to not over-promise or over-hype the product, person or message. The Boy Who Cried Wolf is a useful tale to have in the back of your mind as you package your story. For example, if your in-depth study into the effects of a particular food or drink does not actually show it can help you lose weight, stave off cancer or lengthen your life, then the news release must not give that impression. This is especially true if the study was of rats, not humans.

How to conduct briefings

A briefing is simply telling journalists information you want to appear in the public domain because it helps your cause.

This can be done either on the phone or face-to-face, and with one journalist or several.

A telephone briefing must be conducted at a time when the journalist has no immediate deadline looming. A face-to-face briefing can be done over drinks or a meal, lunch being a favourite. The trick is to have a decent story to give the journalist – they hate having their time wasted, and they may have to justify the time away from the office.

If you can throw in some gossip and titbits of information, that will make the encounter more successful. It is a good idea to have a 'leave-behind' – information in written form or the promise of an email. If you are briefing something and you don't want to be identified as the source, don't be seen in a visible place, such as the Despatch Box coffee bar in Portcullis House.

By the way, that's a good place to watch the briefing process at work, if you ever get the chance. A columnist and a spin doctor have a coffee. A couple of days later, a column appears, favourable to the spin doctor's cause. You can trace the link between one and the other.

How to use pictures

Spin doctors have long understood the potential of visual images to shape our perceptions. That's why they have long sought to get their bosses in photographs which convey deeper meaning.

Martin Rosenbaum in *From Soapbox to Soundbite* says: 'Photo opportunities work by fostering impressions. They do not assert clear propositions which can be the focus of argument, they establish connotations and communicate subliminally.'

Consider the impact of the famous images of Margaret Thatcher riding on a Challenger tank in 1986, with the Union Jack fluttering behind her. She looked, according to the Daily Telegraph, like a 'cross between Isadora Duncan and Lawrence of Arabia'.

The image of African-American athletes Tommie Smith and John Carlos raising their fists in a power salute at the 1968 Olympics remains a powerful symbol of resistance, as does the horrific image of a priest setting himself on fire in 1963 in a protest against the Vietnamese government.

The images of Gordon Brown and Tony Blair sharing ice creams during the 2005 general election in a marginal seat give the impression of unity, while underneath we know the relationship was not so friendly.

Now consider the damage a negative image can do.

Tony Blair took a selfie in front of some naval cadets in 2005. The image was taken and superimposed in front of a burning oil field, making it appear as though Blair was proud of his handiwork. It has been viewed millions of times, including by many whose view of Blair is so warped they assume it's real.

In September 1987, Margaret Thatcher visited Teesside to launch a new regeneration agency. The resulting photos of her alone on post-industrial wasteland had the opposite impact from the one intended. If her image makers wanted to project a story about renaissance they should have had her photographed with people in some hi-tech factory. Instead, the post-industrial wasteland pictures were used to attack her industrial policies.

Or what about the images of Jeremy Corbyn taken in his silver shell suit, or his shorts, looking like a homeless person, or not singing the national anthem? They risk doing irreparable damage to his reputation, more than any extreme policy or manifesto pledge. Remember the images of John Prescott playing croquet? Or the viral video of two Domino's Pizza employees doing unspeakable things to pizzas?

Even the many photographs taken of politicians in front of street names and shop signs which, when cropped a certain way, read as rude words can undermine their credibility or invite ridicule.

Images can do terrible damage to a reputation.

One of the big shifts in the digital revolution is the ability to create and disseminate images and video for next to no cost. The basic rules of picture composition still apply. Journalists still want arresting images which tell a story and draw the reader in. The difference is now these can be generated by anyone with a smartphone, and the internet is awash with them.

To make your package stand out, you need good quality pictures, not ones you've taken on your phone. This may mean commissioning a professional photographer, and developing a series of images which tell your story. A good library of up-to-date images is a worthwhile investment, especially if you can make content available online.

If you are pitching your story to a news desk, you will need high-resolution images capable of being published.

If you are using the photo for your own website or on Twitter, Facebook or Instagram, you should still insist on good quality. As with effective writing, the internet is not an excuse to diminish quality.

How to do stunts

Media stunts are traditionally the preserve of marginal campaign groups who need to do something shocking to gain attention. Perhaps one of the most famous examples of the last twenty years was when a supporter of Fathers4Justice dressed as Batman and scaled the walls of Buckingham Palace. This brought much more public awareness to their campaigning than letter-writing, lobbying or a traditional protest could ever hope to achieve.

Other charities have had more success in using media stunts to garner support for their cause. In 1991, People for the Ethical Treatment of Animals (PETA) launched their 'Rather Go Naked' campaign (with the help of the band The Go-Gos) to protest against the killing of animals to use their fur for clothes. The campaign continues after twenty-five years, having been supported by a range of celebrities including actress Pamela Anderson, pop star Pink and numerous American football players.

On a theme of nudity, in 1999 the Rylstone and District branch of the Women's Institute decided to compile a nude calendar – featuring themselves – with the aim of raising enough money to buy a new sofa for the hospital lounge where one of the members had spent much time in the lead-up to her husband's death of lymphoma.

After coverage from the national press, sales much exceeded the target; to date the calendar has raised over £3 million to fund a new leukaemia and lymphoma research laboratory in Leeds, in addition to the story becoming a feature-length film starring Helen Mirren and Julie Walters, and also a West End musical. This example shows the potential that media stunts have, irrespective of whether your aim is to publicise a large company or a small, local cause with limited funds.

In 2015, Jeremy Clarkson was sacked as presenter of the BBC show *Top Gear* for an 'unprovoked physical attack' on the show's producer, apparently over the lack of a steak after a long day's filming. Snickers posted a picture of a package addressed to Clarkson, featuring their tagline: 'You're not you when you're hungry.' With over 5,000 retweets and the story making it into most of the national newspapers, someone else's unfortunate circumstances clearly make a good basis for a media stunt.

In April 2015, billboards appeared across the TfL network featuring a very slim woman and the tagline 'Are you beach body ready?' The company responsible, Protein World, came under attack from the public for irresponsible advertising and failing to promote positive body image. A protest took place in Hyde Park and the Advertising Standards Authority investigated and banned the billboards from being advertised in their current form.

While this ASA investigation was underway, Carlsberg quickly released a counter-advert asking the public 'Are you beer body ready?' The point of course being that having a Carlsberg required no hard work or preparation whatsoever. In buying up TfL advertising space, Carlsberg were able to ensure that their billboards were placed next to the original ad for Protein World.

With so many examples of positive news coverage from the use of media stunts, it was only a matter of time before politicians tried to get in on the act. The results have usually failed to mirror the success of commercial or campaigners' efforts.

Instead, they have tended to be negative experiences. In 2012, Boris Johnson sought to capitalise on the Olympic spirit by appearing on a zip-wire waving Union Jacks. The images, though, show Johnson suspended in mid-air as the wire got stuck. As David Cameron said afterwards: 'If any other politician anywhere in the world was stuck on a zip-wire it would be a disaster. For Boris, it's an absolute triumph.'

Perhaps the most cringe-worthy political stunt of all time took place in Hastings on 3 May 2015, just days before polling day, when Ed Miliband unveiled a 2.5-metre-tall limestone plinth emblazoned with six election pledges which he told us he would plant in the garden in 10 Downing Street. It was dubbed the Ed Stone, and immediately became a social media viral hit, but not in the way intended.

Of course, any decent spin doctor could have told the Labour team responsible that it looked like an enormous tomb stone (linking in the mind of the public the ideas of Labour, its leader and death), that the wording on the stone bordered on incomprehensible, and that the concept of planting it in the Downing Street garden reeked of hubris. I guess none was available.

The lesson is that the most successful media stunts are low-scale and low-tech and simply rely on the power of retweets to achieve awareness and exposure.

Celebrity endorsement

If you can persuade a celebrity to add their name to your cause, you add newsworthiness to your stories.

Consider how politicians fall over themselves to be associated with film stars or music stars. You can trace it back to Warren Harding's 1920 campaign endorsements by Al Jolson, Douglas Fairbanks and other superstars of the jazz age. In 1960, Kennedy was endorsed by the Rat Pack. Academics have estimated that Oprah Winfrey's endorsement of Barack Obama in the 2008 Democratic primary race was worth one million votes.

As Foreign Secretary, William Hague gained acres more coverage for his campaign to highlight rape used as a weapon of war by collaborating with Angelina Jolie. An international summit to raise the issue, hosted by Hague, cost £5 million, which was about £4 million more than the Foreign Office budget for tackling rape. Not only Angelina but also Brad Pitt turned up, so in spin terms it was worth every penny.

In 2008, the campaign to secure residency rights for former Gurkha soldiers called up one of the biggest guns in the celebrity arsenal: Joanna Lumley. In military terms, that's like deploying, well, the Gurkhas. He father was an officer in the Gurkha Regiment, so she was the perfect celebrity supporter. She set about beating up the Brown government with forceful charm, which drove it to reverse its decision and grant Gurkhas the right to settle in the UK. It is likely that the role of this particular celebrity not only secured media attention, but was decisive in the campaign's victory.

The danger of using celebrities lies in the 'wrong fit' with the cause or message. It makes sense for Jo Brand to endorse a campaign to highlight mental health, because she is a former psychiatric nurse and we know she means it. The endorsement of Russell Brand for Labour in 2015, on the other hand, after he had spent months telling people not to vote, was entirely unhelpful.

But if the celebrity has no known association with the message, it rings untrue. Yardley cosmetics dropped Helena Bonham Carter after she declared she never wore make-up. Worse, if your celebrity endorser suffers a blow to their reputation, it may erode the reputation of your cause or campaign too. OJ Simpson was thrown overboard by Hertz car rental following allegations of domestic abuse (and before his trial for murder).

Surveys

Have you ever noticed that more surveys are reported in summer and over Christmas than any other time of year? This is because a survey is a good method of creating news from nothing, and when news is thin on the ground, a survey can get your story published or broadcast.

Companies often publish surveys in the field of their business: so a building society will publish a survey on first-time buyers, a pensions company will find out about people's savings, a women's mag will survey women about their favourite beauty products, and a condom company will survey young people about their attitudes to sex.

The same guide to news values applies to survey results – so they need to be shocking, surprising, funny or counter-intuitive. If your survey shows that men like football, young people play video games, or older people are concerned about crime, then all you can expect is a chorus of 'so what!'.

Secrets

Lord Northcliffe, newspaper magnate, once said that 'news is what somebody somewhere wants to suppress; all the rest is advertising'.

Ever since Woodward and Bernstein unearthed the Watergate scandal in the early 1970s, journalists have been convinced that government institutions and official agencies are all keeping secrets from us. You can play on this desire to unearth secrets by suggesting your story has something in it that someone somewhere doesn't want published.

The Advertiser, covering north and east Manchester, reported on 4 February 2005 that Tony Blair had been in town. Why was it a front-page story? Here's why:

PM IN SECRET VISIT

THE PRIME Minister took time out of his busy schedule to meet residents at an early morning meeting in Beswick this week.

If the story you're punting has some element of secrecy, it becomes more newsworthy. Journalists love secrets.

Exclusives

The word 'exclusive' appears on so many stories, especially in the tabloids, that the term has become devalued. 'Exclusive' means that the story appears in only the newspaper publishing it.

Because of the intense rivalry between tabloids, the same story can appear in *The Sun* and the *Mirror* as an 'exclusive'. For the spin doctor, an exclusive is a means of giving a story some extra velocity. If a journalist knows they are getting a story on an exclusive basis, they may give it extra prominence.

A strong exclusive story which appears in *The Times* or *Guardian* will generate immediate coverage in that day's radio and television news, and follow-up coverage in the next day's national newspapers. It is important that exclusives are spread around your target media, so that journalists do not become annoyed at being left out. The downside of exclusives is that the journalists you've left in the dark get annoyed.

In his book *Power Trip*, Damian McBride describes giving each lobby journalist a different exclusive ahead of the publication of the budget, so each got a story that no one else had, but also no one got left out.

If you're concerned that your story is a little dull and unlikely to get a journalist interested, you should think about how to apply the X factor – a good photo, a stunt, a survey, a celebrity, or use an exclusive.

Chapter Six

How to Spin in Print

Good stories flow like honey. Bad stories stick in the craw. What is a bad story? It is a story that cannot be absorbed on the first time of reading. It is a story that leaves questions unanswered. It is a story that has to be read two or three times before it can be comprehended. And a good story can be turned into a bad story by just one obscure sentence.

—ARTHUR CHRISTIANSEN, EDITOR OF THE DAILY EXPRESS

The Press, Watson, is a most valuable institution,
if only you know how to use it.

—ARTHUR CONAN DOYLE FROM
THE ADVENTURE OF THE SIX NAPOLEONS

I F YOU WANT to influence journalists, it is not enough to know journalists and to think like journalists. You have to be able to write like journalists. This means that you must be able to churn out accurate, lively copy for newspapers, magazines, websites and broadcasters, in order to get your message into the news.

Here are some of the main formats for presenting your story.

NEWS RELEASES

The news release was always the bog-standard tool of the spin doctor (it should always be called a news release, not 'press release', as this excludes broadcasters), but the digital revolution has made it more or less redundant. Nowadays, you can influence a journalist far more effectively by email or via Twitter.

A news release is a document sent from an organisation to a journalist containing a new story, or useful information, although many organisations use them as a record of their public statements.

The news release is designed to whet a journalist's appetite for more. Given how many millions are produced and pumped out by press offices every year, it is amazing how many are totally rubbish: badly written, wrongly targeted and destined for the waste bin.

Talk to any journalist and they will tell you the huge

proportion of news releases which never get read beyond the first paragraph. Some news releases – addressed to journalists who have died or to magazines which have gone out of business, or offering photo opportunities to LBC – don't even get read.

A news release is geared solely at one audience: the journalist. It has only one purpose: to get the organisation's core messages to target audiences via the media. The issuing of news releases is not a performance indicator nor the end product of media relations, merely a means to an end. You can write all the news releases you like, but if they always end up in the recycling, you're wasting your time.

News releases must contain news

The key to success when writing news releases is to write like the journalist you are targeting. We have seen how news values work, and the sort of stories which appear in the media. The trick is to mould your story into a shape which is recognisable as news.

Like news stories, news releases follow the upside-down pyramid model, with the most newsworthy stuff at the top. The first couple of lines should address the famous five questions:

- Who?
- What?
- Why?
- Where?
- When?

This five-W formula is a useful way of analysing the information you have, focusing the story on the strongest news angle, and dishing up the bare bones of the story without any padding or puffery.

The format of news releases

The format must be consistent and meet journalists' expectations of the information they need. News journalists receive hundreds of news releases every day, and can spare just a few seconds in deciding whether to read them or not. The format for news releases must therefore follow the accepted rules of journalism and transmit the necessary information quickly. Obeying these rules of format and structure is the best way to stand a decent chance of your release being read.

It is a good idea to put the release in the main body of the email, rather than as an attachment, because most news organisations filter out unsolicited attachments, and most people do not open attachments from people they don't know. You can put a logo in the email, and format it to make it look eye-catching.

Date or embargo?

Embargos are used to warn journalists that information issued in advance of an event or announcement cannot be published or transmitted to the public. It is usual for journalists to observe this convention, but if a journalist feels that they can scoop their rivals, and if the source is unimportant enough to risk annoying, they may break the embargo for the sake of the story.

The important thing to understand is that an embargo requests that the journalist doesn't print or broadcast the story, but not that they keep it a secret. I heard of an embargoed news release containing the names of some award winners being sent out from a charity. The journalist phoned the winners ahead of the embargo to see how they felt about winning the award. It was the first they had heard of it.

Who to contact

Contact details with the name of the person journalists should phone and their contact numbers for twenty-four hours should appear at the top as well as at the end of a news release. This is to make the process of follow-up as easy as possible for the journalist, and to ensure that if the news release follows onto a second page, the contact details are not separated and lost.

It is important that the details are correct, and that the person named has not just gone on holiday. If the named contact intends to turn off their phone, they should brief a colleague so that any call from a journalist is not lost.

Ideally, the spin doctor is available for journalists to reach them twenty-four hours a day. News is a 24-hour process, and reporters may well be working on a story late at night on a Sunday for the Monday editions, and bids for interview may come in early in the morning. Indeed, Sunday is a busy day for spin doctors and journalists, preparing for the Monday editions and programmes. Countless opportunities have been lost because a 'contact' was unavailable out-of-hours, and the journalist moved on to another story.

For the attention of...

After the contact details comes the name or place the news release is directed towards. So: 'for the attention of housing correspondents' or 'for news desks' or 'for the attention of forward planning desks'. This helps get the news release into the right person's hands quickly. If you are not sure who the release should be aimed at, put 'for news desks'. It is always best, if possible, to put the name of the actual journalist who will cover the story, which is where building up contacts and researching your target media becomes essential.

Operational note

Occasionally, the news release will not contain news, but information relevant to the operations of a newsroom. For example, that a press officer's mobile number has changed, or that a media event's venue has been moved. In these cases, OPERATIONAL NOTE is written above the heading.

Headline

This is one element of the release which will almost always

be read. Try to tell the story in a few punchy words. Avoid
clever-sounding puns.

Notes to editors

Notes to editors is a convention whereby extra background
information is supplied to journalists. These are numbered,
and the first note will always be the same: the explanation of
what the organisation is and what it does. The second note
might be information about a spokesperson being available
for interview, or that a publication is available on request.
Finally, the news release must end with a contact for more
information, with 24-hour contact numbers.

All of the above advice is just guidance – not all news
releases coming into a newsroom look identical. You should
try to make all your organisation's news releases follow the
same rules, so that journalists feel comfortable with them
and know they will contain the information they need. News
releases are designed to spoon-feed busy journalists and
encourage them to use the information you have sent them.
If the news release is difficult to read or if the story is unclear,
you have failed.

Clearing news releases

Organisations need a clearance procedure for news releases.
This is a necessary process to ensure the release is not
incorrect in the technical details, illegal or untrue. It also

provides a second opinion, and to be honest, covers the back of the spin doctor if something goes wrong. If a news release is issued with incorrect data or a mistake, it is conventional for a second release to be issued, putting right the mistake. This is a real pain in the neck, and can be avoided by getting it right first time.

The clearance process should be as non-bureaucratic and as speedy as possible. It is important for the people who are clearing the release to realise that they are checking for factual errors, not altering style. Journalists will not hang around while six different people, who all think they can write, meddle with your news release. It must be fast.

ARTICLES

Newspapers and magazines publish articles by outside writers. These are sometimes famous celebrities, columnists, politicians or the leaders of organisations with something to say. Getting an article published in a national magazine or newspaper can give your cause or campaign a great boost. It shows that you are serious and that your message is worth listening to. So how is it done?

Ellie Levenson is a writer, publisher and author, and journalism lecturer, who writes pieces for *The Guardian* and *Cosmopolitan*. She says: 'You have to be tenacious, and be prepared to pitch again and again. If you're rejected you have to have a thick skin. Remember, it's the idea that's not right, not you.' She gets ideas from voracious reading of newspapers and magazines. 'I'm not snobby – I read everything from celebrity magazines to broadsheets. Anything can spark an idea. You should be unafraid to write subjects others have covered, because you add a new perspective.'

Reliability is vital. Ellie says: 'If you're asked for 400 words on Wednesday, don't write 800 words on Thursday.'

Many local papers have a 'Soap Box' or 'Your Shout' feature where readers with strong views are invited to submit articles. Often, these slots are hijacked by professional campaigners, but the editors prefer 'real' people with a gripe about a local issue.

Spin doctors are responsible for 'ghosting' articles for their masters. Politicians usually do not have the time nor talent to knock out 300-word articles for tabloids on tackling crime, or education standards, so the task is given to their spin doctors. In the late 1990s, Tony Blair's name frequently appeared on articles in The Sun, Mirror, Express and Daily Mail. You can believe he was a prolific popular journalist during this time, or a more likely explanation, that he employed a team of journalists to ghost-write articles for him.

Feature articles: structure and style

Features allow a greater variety of structures and styles than straight news reporting. There is less pressure to start the article with a hard news intro. The intro can use different devices to draw the reader into the article: humour, teasers, questions, shockers and so on.

There are endless varieties of intros, and with practice, you should deploy different ways of hooking the reader into your article.

Selling in the article

The key target journalist is the features editor, who edits the features section, plans the schedule of articles, commissions writers, and manages in-house writers. This person also has the rotten job of being the target of every freelance, spin doctor and amateur who thought they'd have a go at writing an article about their trip to Corfu. This means they are every bit as harassed by phone calls, unsolicited articles and faxes as news reporters. They appreciate being dealt with in a professional manner, and not pestered.

Before writing an article, you should research your market. Read your target publications carefully. Decide what kinds of articles have been published before. Look at the content, length, tone and style, and emulate it. Write an article which you could easily imagine appearing in your chosen target newspaper or magazine. Getting your article published is known as 'placing' your article.

You can send in your finished article in unsolicited ('on spec') to the features editor, but this is unlikely to be successful. It is possible (I have had a couple of articles in The Guardian which were submitted on spec), but a much better way is to seek agreement from the features editor in advance. You should discuss your idea, perhaps with a brief synopsis, with the features editor, and if they like the idea they will commission you to write the article.

It is usual for non-staff contributors to feature pages to be paid, unlike contributors to news pages. The fee should be agreed in advance. Usually there is a standard rate for the job, based on number of words or 'linage' (number of lines).

There might be a 'kill fee' – a payment paid for a commissioned article which isn't actually published. For working freelance journalists, the point of getting feature articles published is to pay the bills and stop their house contents being repossessed.

For the spin doctor, the point is profile-building or opinion-moulding. This means that the issue of payment is very different for journalists than spin doctors. My view is that when spin doctors offer feature material, they should insist on the going rate for the job. That means the vast PR industry isn't doing journalists out of work, and forcing contribution fees down. You can either keep the cash or give it to charity – it's the principle that counts.

On the other hand, on smaller publications, the fact that spin doctors can offer features without requiring payment gives them the edge over other, competing contributors, and might mean the article is more likely to be published. You must let your conscience decide.

BOOK REVIEWS

Most publications carry reviews of forthcoming books, especially in the trade and technical sector, and reviews can be a good way of getting profile. Publications might have a designated reviews editor who is inundated with review copies of books from publishing houses and their PR agents. These are sent free in the hope that publications will review them, and the book will receive some publicity.

Reviews editors choose their reviewers with care, and try to match the book to the reviewer in a way that will make interesting copy. A biography of a famous politician might be reviewed by another politician who knew him or her well; it might be reviewed by a politician who was their sworn enemy. Either way, the review will have a sharpness and relevance.

Sometimes, established or celebrity reviewers can use the review article almost as a comment piece – using the publication of a new book about cricket to write 300 words on the parlous state of English cricket. If you or your boss is attempting to build a profile as a thinker or authority in a particular area, then reviewing books can help establish a reputation.

You can phone publishing houses and ask the public relations or marketing section for 'review copies' of books, although they will ask for proof of a commission to write a review, or examples of past reviews. If you can swing such proof of genuine intent, you can get hold of most new books as they are launched.

OBITUARIES

Obituaries ('obits') are the articles summing up a noted or famous person's life and activities when they die. National newspapers have obituaries already written for everyone in public life, which are updated regularly. Sometimes, as well as the official obituary, shorter obits can appear by people who knew the person well at a particular time or in a particular field. These can be very personal memories or comments, sometimes simply an anecdote which encapsulated the deceased's personality. Obituaries can be submitted to the obituary editor, and can be a fitting way to pay tribute to a respected figure.

PROFILES

Profiles are the longer articles about a single person, usually a celebrity, and often based on an interview. They tend to appear when celebs have a new book or film to plug. If you or the person you are spinning for is offered the opportunity to be the subject of a profile, jump at it.

These features, always accompanied by a photograph, are the sign that you've arrived, even if it is just in the local paper or trade mag. Here are some more opportunities:

A *Life in the Day* feature, which is a variant on the straightforward profile. Here, a famous person is profiled by concentrating on a typical day in their life.

My favourite books/year/influences are the features where individuals are invited to talk about the books they are taking on holiday, the time in their life they were happiest, who the guiding influences in their lives are, and by revealing this information, we learn a little more about them.

Politicians asked these questions agonise for days over the answers, endeavouring to strike a balance between high-brow and low-brow, between culture and blokeishness. The ultimate torture is *Desert Island Discs*, a seemingly innocuous Radio 4 programme which can make or break reputations far more effectively than *Today*.

'DEAR SIR' – LETTERS TO THE EDITOR

The instantaneous nature of Twitter means that writing letters to newspapers is a dying art. All publications have a letters page where readers are invited to share their thoughts on the world, comment on things they have read, or sometimes appeal for information. They range from the local paper's letters page to the lofty heights of *The Times*, where sometimes letters from the famous and grand become news stories in themselves.

Letters page editors attempt a balance of 'real' people, the great and the good, and people writing on behalf of companies and campaigns. They will also strike a balance between long and short, humorous and serious, and different areas of the country.

Because letters pages are filled with letters from outside, and because a letter can be written and emailed quickly, they can be useful targets for the spin doctor.

Once you've written your letter, it is usually best to email it to the address listed on the letters page itself, but if you're masquerading as a 'real person' posting it might add authenticity. It should be sent on the same day that the publication appears, as early as possible, because 'speed kills'.

HOW TO WRITE LIKE A JOURNALIST

The rules of effective writing apply as much to online platforms as traditional magazines and newspapers. Indeed, the small size of a mobile phone or tablet's screen means that writing should be even more clear, concise and imbued with meaning.

Language must be tailored to the purpose in hand, and this is particularly true of dealing with the media. News releases must emulate in style and content the newspapers at which they are targeted. Feature articles must flow like the articles in that day's papers. They must appear to be crying out for inclusion. It must be easy for the journalist to turn your news release into copy which his or her subs will accept.

A good start is to pay heed to George Orwell's famous advice in his essay 'Politics and the English Language' (1948):

A scrupulous writer, in every sentence he writes, will ask himself at least four questions, thus: 'What am I trying to say? What words will express it? What image or idiom will make it clearer? Is this image fresh enough to have an effect?' And he will probably ask himself two more: 'Could I put it more simply? Have I said anything avoidably ugly?'

The Daily Bulletin

Arthur Christiansen was the editor of the *Daily Express* from 1933 until 1957. Sales of the *Express* under his editorship peaked at four million in 1949. He was a Fleet Street editor of the old school. He expected his editorial staff to have read all the competition by the start of the morning news conference at 11 a.m. All staff had to read all of each edition of the *Express* every day. Every day he issued a bulletin to his journalists, with his instructions on how to make tomorrow's paper better. Here are some of them:

Ban the word 'exclusive' in the *Express*. Our aim is to make everything exclusive. Therefore we have no need to boast.

A story starts 'Remember the story...' The word 'story' should not be used because it is a journalistic phrase. 'Remember the news' is correct. Our readers do not talk about stories but 'articles' or 'pieces' in the paper.

Let us make war on adjectives. The first edition Diary today says that Miss Bridge is 'a well-known flower painter.' There is no need for the adjective. If she is not a well-known flower painter, then the adjective is a lie.

'Once Britten twice shy' is a pun that will amuse some people and irritate others. We should rigorously, vigorously ban puns in headline and text.

We have a rule in the office, which I thought everyone knew, that football clubs are the one exception to our rule that collective nouns take the singular.

We do not like sentences beginning with the word 'Because...' because such sentences confuse the readers. I think we might avoid beginning sentences with the word 'so'.

One thing in particular drives me frantic in newspapers. It is the misplaced crosshead or the misplaced decorative drop letter. Example: On today's first-class leader page there is an enormous drop letter in Jaffa's article right in the middle of a letter from a reader.

It always gives me pleasure when the *Daily Express* has a different lead story of value and worth from the other papers.

Mr Hearst says that his ideal newspaper is one that causes the following reaction: 'When the reader looks at Page One, he says, 'Gee-whiz.' When he turns to the second page, he says, 'Holy Moses.' And when he turns to the middle page, he says, 'God Almighty.'

If you are focusing on a particular newspaper or magazine, you should write in the style of that publication. Many publications, for example the *Financial Times* or *Economist*, publish their own 'style guides' which give comprehensive advice on how they want their English written, with particular emphasis on spelling, punctuation and grammar. These cover all the grey areas not covered by the formal rules of punctuation, grammar and spelling. Style guides can help you with things such as the use of accents on foreign words, Americanisms, capitals or lower case, captions, dates, numbers, foreign words, places, names, government and politics, hyphens, initials, italics, jargon, measures and spelling.

You can pick these up in most decent second-hand book-shops, or buy them new. Some are available for free online, such as *The Guardian*'s and the BBC's. On Twitter, you can follow @guardianstyle for frequent tips and for advice on questions of style.

The aim here is to write copy so utterly compatible with the publication's own style that it can be used almost word-for-word, getting your message in print, and at the same time providing a useful service to the hard-pressed journalist.

The joy of the English language is that it draws on the many linguistic tributaries which have flowed into it down the centuries. It is the product of ancient Greek and Latin, Norman French, Germanic languages and bits and bobs begged, borrowed and stolen from across the globe. That's one reason there are so many words in it (anywhere between 170,000 and over a million, depending on who you believe). Our language is a product of our history.

What this means, though, is that there are inconsistent rules, illogicality and tiresome quirks. Whatever rules you were taught at school, for example 'i before e except after c', are fine except for all the exceptions, such as:

- Either
- Foreign
- Forfeit
- Heifer

- Leisure
- Neither
- Seize
- Sovereign
- Weird

There are many different ways to say the same thing. An academic, a bureaucrat, a scientist and a journalist could all write about the same thing using completely different structure, grammar and vocabulary. So the spin doctor needs to write like the journalist, which means observing the 'ABC': accuracy, brevity and clarity.

How to be accurate

What you write must be right. If a spin doctor is exposed peddling falsehoods, it will be their undoing. But the same applies if what they write is unintentionally inaccurate because of sloppy research, out-of-date figures or false information; it will undermine their credibility just as surely. Any fact or figure can be checked by thousands of readers, and if it appears incorrectly, you will soon know about it.

In January 2016 the Home Office issued a news release about new demands by ministers that Muslim women should learn to speak English, or face deportation. The tough stance was undermined somewhat by the misspelling in the release of the word 'language' as 'langauge'.

How to spell

It's not enough to merely avoid embarrassing gaffes like the one mentioned above. It's also vital to spell correctly to engender trust and confidence in your material.

This is especially true of people's names and where people live. If they live in Middlesbrough, don't write Middlesborough. If you're writing to someone called Alistair, don't call him Alastair. If you think it doesn't matter, ask Alastair Campbell or Alistair Darling.

There are many words which are frequently misspelled. You probably know if there are words you stop and think about. Here are some of the more common ones (according to Wynford Hicks in his excellent *English for Journalists*):

- Abhorrence
- Annihilate
- Authoritative
- Connoisseur
- Corroborate
- Definitely
- Descendant
- Embarrass
- Fallacious
- Harass
- Innocuous
- Jeopardise

- Liaison
- Mantelpiece
- Minuscule
- Noticeable
- Omitted
- Pseudonym
- Reconnaissance
- Restaurateur
- Resuscitate
- Supersede
- Targeted
- Unforeseen
- Vacillate

You're smart enough to know that you can't rely on spell checks. Even if it's set to British not American English, and you avoid all those organizations and programs, it still won't spot words which are really words but not the words you meant, for example:

The minster unveiled the plague at the pubic playing fields.

Minster, plague and pubic are all real words; they're just not the words you wanted to use. Until spell check develops artificial intelligence and knows what you mean, the best advice is to not use it.

The solution lies in buying a good English dictionary, checking every word if you're not sure, and definitely not cutting and pasting other people's material into your document with all of their errors.

How to punctuate

There are plenty of people in the world who will think less of you if you mangle your punctuation. Punctuation is a series of symbols which are aimed to help the reader understand clearly what you mean. Many people consider punctuation to be a series of arcane rules designed to catch you out.

The spin doctor's best friend is the full stop. This is because it shows that you have come to the end of a sentence containing one clear idea. This suggests some clear thought has gone into your writing.

Other marks of punctuation such as commas, parentheses, dashes, semi-colons or colons suggest that you have just thought of something else to add into your sentence, and it elongates with each new thought, added on without any clear end in sight, as the words come tumbling freely, unthinkingly and without thought of the poor reader, like a stream of consciousness (and your work ends up like a novel by James Joyce).

The one that really bugs people is the apostrophe, which shows that something is missing ('That's a great hat.') or something belongs to something or someone ('The boy's hat is red.')

The common mistakes are confusing its and it's (which can set some people off like a firework), or worse, the so-called 'grocers' apostrophe' which is the insertion of apostrophes into plural words such as banana's or apple's for no reason at all.

An area of controversy in the world of apostrophes is when the word ends in the letter s. So for example St James' Park or St James's Park? Both are right, but which one you choose will depend on 'house style'.

Be careful of apostrophes in brand names. If the company has decided whether and where the apostrophe comes in their brand name, that's what you run with. For example:

- Sainsbury's
- Waterstones
- Standard and Poor's
- Starbucks
- Barclays
- McDonald's
- Kellogg's
- Tesco

What about place names? Again, you just have to adopt the accepted use, no matter how annoying, for example:

- King's Cross
- St John's Wood
- Barons Court

And the town I grew up in, Gerrards Cross (is he?).

And never, ever confuse Queens' College, Cambridge (founded by two queens) and The Queen's College, Oxford (founded to honour one queen).

Other marks of punctuation include the exclamation mark! This should never be used by spin doctors, no matter how exciting you consider your writing. It is like laughing at your own joke. The exception here is informal writing such as texts or tweets, and names which include it, such as Yo! Sushi (the restaurant chain); Westward Ho! (a seaside village in Devon named after the novel by Charles Kingsley, and the only place in the UK with an exclamation mark); and *Very Good, Jeeves!* (a series of short stories by P. G. Wodehouse).

How to be grammatical

Grammar, like spelling and punctuation, is there to help you. You have to obey the basic rules, so that sentences have subjects, verbs and objects which all match up.

One of George Orwell's tips for writers was to use the active voice rather than the passive voice. All this means is to start with the subject, then the verb, then the object:

The Minister knocked over a fence with his scooter.

Rather than the passive voice which would be:

A fence was knocked over by the Minister with his scooter.

The point is that the active voice contains some energy and zip which carries the reader along, whereas the passive voice creates a damp lettuce leaf of a sentence. It also creates the opportunity for faceless bureaucracies, or those seeking to avoid blame, to leave out the subject, and avoid any responsibility for their actions:

It was decided that a new sewage treatment plant would be built at the end of the garden

Dad, the window next door has been broken by a football.

Spin doctors are often dealing with organisations which are singular but made up of individual people. So you need to get the grammar right on nouns such as:

- Team
- Cabinet
- Government
- Committee
- Board

Is it 'The Cabinet is deciding whether to bomb Syria', or 'The Cabinet are deciding whether to bomb Syria'? The advice here is that you should treat it as a singular, with verbs which 'agree', for example:

The United Nations (UN) is debating the issue tomorrow.

The rules of grammar do not apply to speech-writing, which is a form of poetry, and relies on the sounds, metre and rhetorical flourishes of the spoken word, rather than sentence construction. Thus you can have verbless sentences.

There are other areas which you should endeavour to get right. These are the things that matter a great deal to some people, and it's best not to inadvertently annoy them. Here's a few of my favourites:

Fewer and Less. It's 'fewer' if you can count it, and 'less' if you

can't. So: there are fewer poor households, and less poverty.
When you go to the supermarket, you can feel smug when you see
the sign saying 'Ten Items or Less' in the knowledge it should be
'fewer'. Unless you're in Waitrose, where it says 'fewer'.

Unique. If it's the only one in existence, then it's unique.
Otherwise it's not. It can't be a bit unique, virtually unique or
pretty much unique. There are no degrees of uniqueness.

Writing **disinterested** when you mean 'uninterested'.

A **crescendo** is a steady build-up of something, usually music.
It is not a peak, climax or apex.

Gambit means the opening move in a game of chess. So a gambit
is always the first move. You don't need to say 'opening gambit.'

Light years measure distance not time.

You can only have two **alternatives.** More than two, and they
become choices or options.

And never say '**literally**' when you mean 'figuratively'. Your sides
did not literally split because you were laughing so much.

How to be brief

Journalists, as we have seen, are busy people, inundated with
information by those hoping to attract their attention. The art of

journalism is conveying meaning through the concise use of the right words in the right order. So must it be for the spin doctor.

Tony Blair, reflecting on his time as Prime Minister, wrote:

The way in which information is exchanged so quickly has forever changed the way in which people want to consume information. They demand that things be condensed into 20-second sound bites. With complex problems, this is exceedingly difficult, but to be an effective communicator and leader you need to be able to condense complex items down to the core and be able to do this quickly.

It's not that new a phenomenon. Winston Churchill insisted on short, sharp memoranda which got to the point and had a clear purpose. These suggested that the writer had done the heavy lifting of discussion and thought, and boiled the information and advice down to the bare bones.

This takes confidence, because it involves leaving information out. It means distinguishing between what the person must be told, what they should be told, and what they could be told, with the 'coulds' cut out.

Have in your mind the 'KISS' principle: Keep It Short and Simple. (Or Keep It Simple, Stupid.)

This means:

- short words (one or two syllables wherever possible)
- short sentences (around ten words)
- short paragraphs (around five lines)
- short documents (on one side if you can manage it)

Writing a short, sharp document is harder than writing a long, rambling one. If you were asked to write 3,000 words on the workings of the European Union, you could knock it up in half an hour. It would be rubbish, probably, but you could do it. Now try writing eighty words on the workings of the European Union, which can be read and understood by 12 million people over their breakfast.

The best way to be brief is to be clear about what you want to say, and that means thinking before you write. Everyone, once commissioned to write something, is tempted to start tapping away at the keyboard. This leads to sloppy writing, because you are thinking and writing simultaneously. It leads to long sentences and long paragraphs.

Far better is to think, plan, research and discuss first, then get it down on paper. Once you start writing it is a good idea to keep going. Don't stop to check facts and figures. This will interrupt your flow, and make you forget where you were heading next.

The poet Coleridge was famously interrupted in the midst of writing 'Kubla Khan', which had come to him in a dream, by a person from the village of Porlock knocking on his door. When Coleridge returned to his desk, he had forgotten the rest of the poem.

George Orwell advised us to 'never use a long word if a short word will do'.

The Economist Style Guide says: 'Short words: Use them. They are often Anglo-Saxon rather than Latin in origin. They are easy to spell and easy to understand.'

Be strict with yourself. If you come across a Latinate word in your writing, dripping with syllables fresh from the mouth of a Roman centurion, replace it with a short, sharp Anglo-Saxon equivalent. Remove facilitate, participate, accommodate or terminate, and replace with help, join in, house or stop.

Most importantly, read through your material and be ruthless in the editing. Take a scalpel to it and cut out the tumours of wasted words, redundant phrases and pointless tautology. Arthur Quiller-Couch, in his 1914 lecture on writing style, said: 'Whenever you feel an impulse to perpetrate a piece of exceptionally fine writing, obey it – whole-heartedly – and delete it before sending your manuscript to press. *Murder your darlings.*'

How to be clear

Clarity of writing comes from clarity of thought. The spin doctor needs to understand what they are trying to communicate, and why. A spin doctor should be a wordsmith, but first comes a clear understanding of what you're trying to achieve, which is shared across the organisation.

Effective writing should be based on the simple idea that the writer can write something which the reader can read once and understand. That sounds obvious, and yet seems beyond the ability of virtually every corporate copywriter, government department, bank, university, hospital or local council.

Instead, we are drowned in a sea of jargon. Jargon is not necessarily a bad thing. When used among members of the same trade, profession or sub-culture, it allows them to communicate ideas quickly. Doctors, journalists, politicians, software engineers, taxi drivers and hairdressers all have their own jargon.

The problem is when jargon seeps out into the mainstream world, and pollutes the atmosphere with meaningless, annoying phrases.

Management-speak rests almost entirely on meaningless phrases:

- Blue-sky thinking
- Pushing the envelope
- Boil the ocean
- Helicopter view
- Open the kimono
- Low-hanging fruit

I even recently heard someone use, with a straight face, the expression 'we need to de-room this elephant'.

Jargon is used to make organisations and their products sound sophisticated, to make individuals sound knowledgeable, and to bamboozle unwitting members of the public. This should be anathema to a spin doctor, for whom the important thing is a clear message, succinctly delivered.

Acronyms and initials

What's the difference? An acronym is a word made from initials which is pronounced as though it was a word, such as:

IKEA   (Ingvar Kamprad Elmtaryd Agunnaryd)

NATO   (North Atlantic Treaty Organization)

UNICEF   (United Nations International Children's
          Emergency Fund)

DECC   (Department for Energy and Climate Change)

Sometimes the acronym is used so frequently, it evolves into a word, and the original meaning is forgotten:

Radar   (radio detection and ranging)

Laser   (light amplification by stimulated emission of radiation)

Scuba   (self-contained underwater breathing apparatus)

Initials are shorthand for a longer series of words, but each letter is enunciated, for example BBC, WTO, UN or NHS.

If the initials are very well-known (BBC) you can get away with using them. If not, you should spell out the name in full the first time you use it, and then use the initials from then on. Never use initials without explaining them, especially if they have more than one meaning:

PR: public relations, proportional representation

PC: politically correct, police constable, personal computer

SME: small and medium enterprise, subject matter expert

I pity the US Army spin doctor who had to explain this piece of nonsense uttered by General Schwarzkopf during the first Gulf War: 'It is not yet possible to get clear BDA in this area of the KTO. The continued presence of Triple A means a constant risk of allied personnel becoming KIA or WIA.'

How to proofread

Proofreading is the art of spotting the mistakes which inevitably creep into a document. As we have seen, this process needs to be extremely rigorous to avoid embarrassing errors.

Proofreaders are one of the specialist trades in the printing and publishing industry, checking the 'galley proofs' (the first typeset version of a publication) for accuracy. Proofreading involves a series of marks on the page which denote instructions to the typesetters, such as a squiggle underneath a word to show it should be in bold, or a cross in a circle to show the text should be changed to the correct font.

The problem is that if you're editing your own material, your brain plays tricks on you. You read what you know you wrote, not what is actually on the page in front of you. There are various methods to increase the likelihood of spotting errors:

Get someone else to read it. This is the most effective, because the other person will not know what you meant to write. They will read what is there on the page.

Print it off. If you read the page in natural light, not from a backlit screen, it is easier to spot mistakes.

Sleep on it. If you can build in some time between writing and proofreading, you will spot more mistakes. In a time-pressured environment, this might only be the time it takes to get a coffee, but it will still create some space between writing and proofreading.

Read it backwards. This takes each word away from its neighbours, and decontextualising it makes it easier to check each word for accuracy.

Read it aloud. Some people swear by this, because it allows you to check for accuracy, especially grammar. Reading aloud forces you to slow down, so you're more likely to spot errors. If you're not reading aloud, you're more likely to skim-read.

Proofreading is not the same as sub-editing or copy-editing; it is just about getting it right, not length or style.

How to avoid clichés

You should avoid clichés like the plague.

You should avoid acid test, bitter end, burning issue, crying need, dead as a dodo, dark horse, horns of a dilemma, last but not least, sea of faces, take the bull by the horns, or this day and age.

If you can't give clichés a wide berth, steer clear of them, then rope in some other Joe to put pen to paper.

Incidentally, Robert Hutton, political reporter for *Bloomberg News*, has written a great book, *Romps, Tots and Boffins*, which highlights the clichés, as well as the jargon words and phrases used by journalists, to create 'journalese'.

How to structure your argument

Spin doctors, like journalists, need to structure their messages based on the model of the upside-down pyramid. This is the first thing you learn at journalism school. The idea is that you take the mass of information you have, and break it down into:

- Who
- What
- Why
- Where
- When
- (and sometimes How)

You then reassemble the information with the most interesting of the five Ws at the start. This is the widest part of the upside-down pyramid.

The first paragraph from this sad story in the *Sunday Express* (2 January 2005) is a good example:

Boy, 8, dies as gales hit Britain

A BOY of eight died as wintry storms lashed Britain yesterday.

Who? A boy of eight.

What? He died.

Why? Because of wintry storms.

Where? Britain.

When? Yesterday.

In the middle of the article come secondary facts, and at the bottom comes added colour, texture, background and quotes. This is how journalists construct news stories, and therefore how you should structure your news releases, briefings, 'top lines' for broadcast interviewees, or other materials aimed at journalists.

The idea is that if the reader doesn't get that far, there is no new or mind-blowing information buried at the bottom. Also, if the article is edited for space, the sub will cut from the bottom upwards, often without even reading what is being discarded.

People fresh from academia or other walks of life find this hard, because they have often been trained to use the opposite structure, with the document leading the reader on a journey of discovery, by way of this or that argument and discussion, reaching a dramatic conclusion at the end. Journalism is the opposite. You give away the best stuff at the beginning.

Chapter Seven

How to Spin on the Air

Television? No good will come of this device.
The word is half Greek and half Latin.

—C. P. SCOTT

BROADCASTERS NEED PEOPLE to give interviews on their programmes. More broadcasters and more programmes mean more people are needed to give more interviews. This presents spin doctors with a huge opportunity, and also a huge threat. On radio and television, reputations can be made or broken. An interview gone wrong is no longer a fleeting moment of embarrassment.

It can be tweeted around the globe in minutes, reaching audiences way beyond the numbers of people watching or listening to the programme. And, of course, it remains online for the rest of time.

Andy Warhol said that in the future everyone would be famous for fifteen minutes. In 2006 that was proved correct when Guy Goma was interviewed on the BBC News channel about a court case involving Apple. The problem was that Guy Goma was a graduate from Congo who was waiting in the Television Centre reception to be interviewed for a job before being whisked into the studio, and the real interviewee, Guy Kewney, was left waiting.

Radio and TV remain powerful media, which have a huge reach and credibility, and can help you get your message across to millions. A good clip on the news can be sent to your target audiences via YouTube or Twitter, and live on your website long after the actual broadcast.

There remains a glamour about appearing on the news or being interviewed in a studio. If you've ever done it, you'll find that people come up to you for days afterwards saying 'I saw you on the TV'.

Many spin doctors produce their own videos, with their spokespeople appearing in short films uploaded onto websites and disseminated via social media. These can be of varying quality. On 12 May 2015, Chuka Umunna MP went to Swindon to make a three-minute film announcing his intention to run for the leadership of the Labour Party. The picture quality looked like it was filmed on a phone, and the audio quality sounded like it was recorded at sea. It may have been intended to look gritty and authentic, but to many it looked a bit ropey. The main advantage of making your own films is editorial control, but the downside is your self-produced interview is unlikely to reach the size of audience, or have the authenticity you need to shift public opinion.

There's some great advice lifted from television comedy *Yes Minister*, written in the late '70s and early '80s about how to run a television broadcast:

> If you're changing a lot of things, you want to look reassuring and traditional. Therefore you should have a dark suit and an oak-panelled background and leather books. But if you're not doing anything new, you'd want a light modern suit and a modern high-tech setting with abstract paintings.

And as for the music? 'Bach for new ideas; Stravinsky for no change.'

There are hundreds of broadcast outlets which might bid for you to appear, depending on who you are and what you're saying.

There are the big, prestigious programmes such as BBC Two's *Newsnight*, or BBC Radio 4's *Today* programme, which are considered to shape the news agenda. There are the daytime TV breakfast shows. There are local radio and TV stations. There are stations such as Russia Today or Press TV, which are the state broadcasters for Russia and Iran respectively, and which you may want to avoid if you have a conscience.

There are two reasons why you might be asked to do an interview: first, because you are the originator of news and the interview is about you, your organisation, your latest report, or whatever. Second, because the news story is about an issue in which you have a direct interest, and you are asked for comment, or expert opinion.

The request from broadcast journalists (known as a 'bid') to appear usually comes with only a few hours' notice. It often means being in a radio studio at some unearthly hour of the morning, or else in a TV studio late at night. A spin doctor needs to work to the broadcasters' timetables, not their own, and that means lots of late nights, early mornings and week-ends. The role of the spin doctor is often to explain this to their clients or bosses.

The broadcasters will try to make the whole experi-ence as easy as possible – but the days of free cars, food in the green room and lavish appearance fees have largely disappeared. Some will send a car for you, and if you merit it, they may send a broadcaster to you to record the interview.

The BBC in the south-east despatched a reporter to my home recently. She appeared at my door, on her own, asked the questions, filmed the interview, edited it on her Apple Mac using video editing software and uploaded the film to her newsroom, where it was dropped into a news package and broadcast forty minutes later. In the 1970s, a TV news crew might comprise five or six people, and films would be sent to the studio via motorcycle couriers.

FIELDING THE BID

When the bid comes in, you have to make a snap decision whether or not to take part. Will your appearance help or hinder your cause? A senior PR person recounted to me recently how their client, following an air disaster, was lined up for the Today programme and other major news programmes. The PR man's advice was to withdraw the offer and not take the immediate heat. It turned out to be good advice. The point is, just because a prestigious show calls you up, you don't have to appear if it would make things worse.

You need to ascertain key information from the caller (usually a researcher or production assistant). Here's what you need to know:

- What is the programme?

- Is it live or pre-recorded?

- When does it go out?

- Why have they asked you?

- Who else is appearing?

- Has something happened to provoke the story (a new report you haven't read)?

- How long is the piece?

- Who is conducting the interview?

- What will the line of questioning be?

What you can't ask is 'what are the questions?', nor can you start to lay down the law about when and how the interview will take place.

If the interview is just you and the interviewer, it is known as a 'one plus one'. If it's with you, the interviewer and someone else, it is a one plus two. The interview may be conducted remotely, with you sitting in a mini studio at 4 Millbank or the regional BBC studio on your own.

On radio, the interview might be conducted over a landline phone, over an ISDN line, or from another studio. Some broadcasters use Skype. If the editor thinks you're worth it, you might end up in a 'radio car' – a kind of mobile studio in a van which comes direct to you.

On television, they might conduct an interview live from another studio or from a location. If the interview is pre-recorded for television, a certain amount of trickery is involved. The crew will only have one camera, so they will film the interviewer asking the questions and nodding at your answers (a 'noddy') separately, and edit it in afterwards.

Some broadcasters still like a walking set-up shot, with you strolling through a park or up some stairs, or a set-up shot of you pretending to write something at a desk, or taking a book off a shelf and looking at it in a studious manner. These are clunky reminders of the old days before digital broadcasting. *Newsnight*, for example, has banned walking set-ups, but still uses noddies.

The most important question for you is 'live or pre-recorded?'. This information is the most important element of the interview, and changes your whole approach. A live interview is high-risk. Live interviews can be terrifying – even the most seasoned operators are tested by the likes of Jeremy Paxman or John Humphrys. I've been interviewed by both, and it is a scary experience. Make a mistake, and everyone sees or hears it. On Twitter, no one can hide.

Green Party leader Natalie Bennett appeared on the Nick Ferrari show in February 2015 and suffered a 'brain fade'. She couldn't answer questions about her own party's spending plans, and soon the clip was being circulated across social media. The advantage to a live interview is that you are in control, you can't be edited, and if you get your message across, it will be broadcast.

If the interview is a short clip pre-recorded, it means you can make a mistake and try again. Very occasionally, the broadcaster will use the mistake if your discomfort adds to their story.

For example, in 2009, the chief executive of the British Dental Association (BDA), Peter Ward, conducted a pre-recorded interview for ITV's *Tonight* programme, on mercury in dental fillings. When the interviewer's questions became a little searching, Mr Ward waved his hands in the air and went 'lalalalalalala'. Presumably, he thought that would render the interview unusable, but instead it was broadcast, watched by millions of bemused viewers. If you want to shudder with embarrassment, take a look on YouTube.

The next day he issued the following statement on the BDA website:

Many of you will have watched the *Tonight* programme 'What's in your mouth?'. For those who did (and indeed those who didn't) I must offer my full and unmitigated apologies for my performance. The scenes that were broadcast represent a small fraction of the interview that did not follow the sequence I expected and caught me by surprise. That is, however, no excuse for the spoiling tactics I adopted on the spur of the moment. To my colleagues, I would like to say that I am truly sorry.

A word of warning – be clear what kind of interview you're doing. A famous clip of John Prescott involved him doing a TV interview with Nick Robinson, stopping himself halfway through an answer, complaining that 'that was crap', and then being informed that the interview was live. Both Prescott and Robinson were barely able to contain their laughter.

When the interview is pre-recorded you can take your time to prepare and get it right. On pre-recorded radio, you will be asked to 'give some level', so the technicians can hear your voice and set their equipment. You normally get asked to say what you had for breakfast. This is a good opportunity to get used to the microphone and relax your voice. It is usually a good idea to drink some water just before speaking, because fear will work to dry your mouth.

Despite the perfectly natural pants-wetting terror that appearing on radio and TV induces in most people, and the ever-present danger of making a fool of yourself in front of millions of strangers, there are tried and tested techniques which can help things go smoothly and provide reassurance.

HOW TO PREPARE

Preparation is the key to a successful interview. You must think it through in advance and practise what you want to say.

You should also identify weak spots in your argument and be prepared to answer hostile questions, although most interviewers are not trying to deliberately trip you up.

Write down your key points and rehearse them out loud. The sound of an answer is very different from how it appears on paper.

You need to have decided what your key message, or 'top line', is. This is the thing you want people to hear (and what you will kick yourself about afterwards if you fail to get across).

Kate Dixon, a radio producer for BBC political programmes, advises:

> Succinct, knowledgeable and human; making points in a passionate and memorable way are the ingredients of a good interview. Facts and figures are a great part of an interviewee's armoury – but they must be accurate, and use them with maximum impact. Don't just say 15,000 people are unemployed in Lambeth – say that's one in five of the working population.

The first question is usually a straightforward, scene-setting question, to allow you to get your point of view across. Think of this as the 'what's your favourite colour' question.

The trick is the second and subsequent questions: 'why do you say "blue" when only last week you said it was "red"?'

You should always prepare for the worst possible question, and try out some answers. If you can think of the worst question, so can the presenter.

HOW TO CONSTRUCT YOUR SOUND BITE

When you have decided what you want to say, you need to condense your thoughts into short, sharp digestible chunks, widely known as 'sound bites'. These are the short, snappy and memorable phrases used for radio and TV, repeated on rolling news bulletins, and spread virally on social media. A ten-second clip on Vine or Twitter can reach millions.

'Sound bite' is a term born in the USA, and stems particularly from the 1988 Presidential election between George Bush and Michael Dukakis. As Michael Dukakis, reflecting after the 1998 Presidential election, said: 'If you couldn't say it in less than ten seconds, it wasn't heard because it wasn't aired.'

Sound bites have been denounced as undermining and trivialising the political process by not allowing arguments to be expanded and explained. I disagree. I believe that it is no bad thing if politicians and other public figures are disciplined into encapsulating their message into understandable, coherent phrases. It helps reduce the amount of waffle in the world.

Margaret Thatcher says in her *Downing Street Years* that, before winning the 1979 election, the Tories had 'taken apprenticeships in advertising and learnt how to put a complex and sophisticated case in direct, clear and simple language'. When a politician fails to properly convey his or her meaning, as Gordon Brown did with his phrase 'post-neo-classical endogenous growth theory', they are rightly lampooned.

The sound bite is really only a new version of the slogan – which has been in politics for centuries. Instead of distributing his lengthy political tomes to the Russian masses, Lenin invented a sound bite to encapsulate what the Bolsheviks stood for: 'Bread, peace and land'.

During the 1964 general election campaign, Harold Wilson used to judge the moment in his speeches when the BBC would start to broadcast it live, and switch his remarks to messages which he wanted the viewers to hear, not his party faithful audience.

Your sound bites needn't be candidates for inclusion in the *Oxford Dictionary of Quotations*, but should express your point in words that are memorable, compelling and repeatable. Kate Dixon says: 'Always include a full stop. Finish making a point, never stray into making another one unless you've finished the first. (I had one interview I couldn't edit as the peer never finished her sentence!)'

Great sound bites are short. They are concrete, not abstract. They are visual, so the listener can see what you mean in their own imagination. They may use rhetorical tricks such as alliteration, repetition, clusters of three words or phrases, or rhymes. They hang around in the memory, long after everything else has faded to black.

The users of sound bites should be, as Peggy Noonan has

said, 'simply trying in words to capture the essence of the thought they wished to communicate'.

We all have our favourites. One of mine is Tony Blair's, at the signing of the Good Friday Agreement: 'A day like today is not a day for sound bites, really. But I feel the hand of history upon our shoulders.'

If at all possible, they should be resistant to parody. In *The Thick of It*, the hapless Labour leader Nicola Murray comes up with a range of sound bites which immediately invite ridicule, including 'Fourth Sector Pathfinders' and 'Quiet Batpeople'.

David Cameron's poster slogan in 2010 'We Can't Go On Like This. I'll Cut the Deficit Not the NHS' was spoofed a thousand times.

HOW TO STICK TO YOUR MESSAGE WITHOUT SOUNDING LIKE A ROBOT

One of the things that really annoys an audience is interviewees seeming to ignore or evade a tricky question. They hate people who sound robotic, like they're repeating a prepared script. A CEO appearing just after a major product recall should sound on top of things and truly contrite, rather than like a hostage reading out a statement written by their captors.

Watch an episode of *Gogglebox* when a political interview is on and see how annoyed people get. Asking tricky questions is the journalist's job, but your job is to get a message across. Therein lies the need for the interviewee's skill and dexterity.

One of the first British politicians to properly understand the workings of TV was Labour leader Harold Wilson. According to Gerald Kaufman, his then spin doctor, Wilson

> didn't go to the TV studio to answer the questions. The questions were an irrelevance which had to be listened to ... he decided what he wanted to say – the message he wanted to communicate to the people who were watching and then, regardless of the questions that were put to him, he said what he meant to say.

Similarly, Liberal Democrat peer David Steel admits: 'I always make a habit of writing down three or four points I want to make and proceed to make them regardless of the questions the erudite interrogators or their even more erudite researchers have made up.'

And in the interests of political balance, here's former Tory Prime Minister Edward Heath: 'The thing to do before a big programme is to be clear in your mind about what you want to say, because the interviewer will always try and deal with something else.'

The problem with this old-school method is that people are wise to it, and it sounds like you're avoiding the question. You need to sound like you are answering the question, while getting your point across.

One method used by successful interviewees is the ABC technique:

- Acknowledge
- Bridge
- Communicate

You acknowledge the question, but then use a linking phrase to bridge onto the thing you really want to say:

A: 'That's an important question, and we're addressing it'

B: 'but what really matters right now'

C: 'is that we continue to do X, Y and Z.'

Tune into some interviews on radio and TV, and you'll hear it being used.

HOW TO SOUND AUTHENTIC

The way people get their point across in broadcast interviews is changing fast. People crave easy-going authenticity, and that takes a lot of effort. The days of just repeating your message over and over are gone.

For decades, spin doctors told their clients: stick to your message; don't be distracted. That ended in June 2011 when Ed Miliband conducted what the *New Statesman* has branded one of the top five worst political interviews. The topic of the ill-fated conversation between him and ITV's north of England correspondent Damon Green was a public sector strike. During this short interview, Miliband was asked five different questions. Unfortunately, he had his pre-agreed lines, and stuck admirably to them. Each answer was a variant on the following theme:

> These strikes are wrong at a time when negotiations are still going on. Parents and the public have been let down by both sides, because the government has acted in a reckless and provocative manner. After today's disruption, I urge both sides to put aside the rhetoric, get round the negotiating table and stop it happening again.

Charlie Brooker wrote in *The Guardian*: 'It sounds like an interview with a satnav on a roundabout.'

The episode was only made worse by the fact that ITV had agreed to pool this interview with BBC and Sky for their news programmes. With average combined viewing figures of approximately 15 million for their 6 p.m. bulletins, a quarter of the population sat down after work to watch what was, by any measure, a complete PR disaster.

For those that missed it on TV, Damon Green uploaded the footage to YouTube along with an angry tweet criticising Miliband and his PR team. To date, the video has over half a million views.

HOW TO LOOK

If appearing on TV, appearance matters. On radio, no one can tell what you look like. Television is the most powerful medium, and people tend to remember what interviewees look like, not what they say. That means that smart unassuming business-like clothes and a clean, kempt appearance are essential. If you want to be persuasive you should look credible. As the anti-apartheid leader Steve Biko once said: 'If you want to say something radical, you should dress conservative.'

Kennedy is widely assumed to have beaten Nixon in the 1960 Presidential election TV debate not because of policy differences, but because Nixon looked dishevelled, sweaty, unshaven and shifty, and Kennedy wore full make-up and looked smooth and trustworthy. The radio audience, who only heard the debate, overwhelmingly voted Nixon the winner.

Many spokespeople who might expect bids from television at the last moment keep an ironed white shirt and tie, or blouse and jacket, in their office just in case.

It is normal for men appearing on TV to use make-up – usually some powder to take away shiny foreheads and five o'clock shadows, and disguise bags under the eyes. In studio interviews, the interviewee is taken to make-up beforehand. For interviews outside at your own location, the TV crew will not have any make-up.

If seated for a TV interview, sit on the back of your jacket to stop it riding up and making you look hunch-backed. Straighten your tie if you have one on. Avoid distracting jewellery, flashy ties or waistcoats. If you want what you have to say to be taken seriously, look sober and respectable, and if you want people to listen to your message, then avoid distractions like wild hand-gestures and violent nods of the head.

HOW TO MOVE

Your posture and body language are as important as what you say. You must try (and it is very hard) to control your non-verbal communication. Sit up straight, smile, maintain eye contact, and keep your hands and feet still. Control your breathing.

If you are addressing a serious subject, look serious. Do not allow a smile to dance across your lips if you are dealing with significant job losses or an outbreak of E. coli.

Avoid the 'foot-flap' – the non-verbal signal for 'I want to get out of here'. Don't shuffle about in your seat, because that makes you look uncomfortable and shifty. Don't close your eyes for longer than a blink or touch your nose when answering, because that implies you are lying or have something to cover up.

HOW TO AVOID TRAPS

Appearing on radio or TV, even a local station, can have a huge impact. If you do it, you will be surprised how many people comment on your appearance afterwards. If you really mess it up, you will star on YouTube for years to come, and be used by people like me as examples of how not to do it.

You should be keen, therefore, to avoid the pitfalls.

Never lose your temper (although a good interviewer might try to make you lose your rag; it makes great TV). You should be polite, but firm, and try to get the last word. You should try to use the interviewer's name, but only once (any more and it becomes a distraction or sounds obsequious, or even insulting to the interviewer).

BE CAREFUL AROUND MICROPHONES

If you're near a microphone, the chances are what you say is being listened to, and recorded. Public affairs are littered with examples of public figures saying stupid things near microphones, unintended for public consumption, which broadcasters gleefully put on air.

Ronald Reagan famously prefaced his weekly radio address in August 1984 with the following sound check: 'My fellow Americans, I'm pleased to tell you today that I've signed legislation that will outlaw Russia forever. We begin bombing in five minutes.'

It wasn't actually broadcast live, contrary to popular myth, but it was widely reported.

In July 1993, the Prime Minister John Major was caught on tape chatting to Michael Brunson before a big ITV interview. He called three of his Cabinet colleagues 'bastards', and earned headlines like this one from The Independent:

Major 'says three in Cabinet are bastards'

JOHN MAJOR's leadership was plunged into a new crisis last night after claims that he described three Eurosceptic Cabinet colleagues as 'bastards' in comments accidentally recorded after a television interview.

There are myriad other examples: Prince Charles being rude about the BBC's royal correspondent Nicholas Witchell ('These bloody people. I can't bear that man. I mean, he's so awful, he really is'), or Deputy Prime Minister Nick Clegg's remark to David Cameron after a joint visit to Boots in Nottingham ('If we keep doing this we won't find anything to bloody disagree on in the bloody TV debate').

A schoolboy error: Gordon Brown and Mrs Duffy

Gordon Brown was never likely to win the 2010 general election. His short-lived government between 2007 and 2010 was beset with a toxic combination of bad luck, poor judgement and public relations disasters. An early decision to call off a general election killed Brown's reputation for political acuity, and the global financial crash damaged his reputation for financial probity. A series of unforced errors, such as the 10p tax fiasco, blighted his months in office. However, during the 2010 election, Brown created a public relations storm to rival Gerald Ratner. On a visit to Rochdale, Brown was introduced in the street to a voter – Gillian Duffy – who had popped out for a loaf of bread. As a life-long Labour voter, she raised some of the issues close to her heart, including immigration. Brown listened and chatted, as the cameras recorded the exchange.

Then disaster struck. Brown was wearing a radio mic which he forgot to take off in his car. Once in the safety of the car, the Prime Minister let rip:

Brown: That was a disaster. Well I just ... should never have put me in with that woman. Whose idea was that?

Aide: I don't know, I didn't see.

Brown: It was Sue [Nye] I think. It was just ridiculous.

Aide: I'm not sure if they [the media] will go with that.

Brown: They will go with that.

Aide: What did she say?

Brown: Oh everything, she was just a sort of bigoted woman. She said she used to be Labour I mean it's just ridiculous.

Sky News broadcast Brown's words within seconds of him delivering them, and then played the tape to Mrs Duffy, who was mortified. It gets worse. The PM's next appearance was on BBC Radio 2's *Jeremy Vine Show*, and Vine played the tape to the PM, who crumpled visibly on hearing his own words. How do we know he crumpled, even though it was on radio? Because most radio stations now have cameras in their studios recording video as well as sound.

Within minutes, the story was rampaging around Twitter and every other social media site.

Peter Mandelson attempted an emollient response to the media: 'For the government and the Labour Party as a whole, we are compassionate people, we care about others like Mrs Duffy, we respect her point of view.'

It was too late. The voters heard a Prime Minister being rude about a pensioner behind her back, and the view that Labour wasn't listening to the people on immigration was cemented in the public's mind.

There are deeper lessons about leadership, trust, empathy and emotional intelligence to be learnt from Gordon Brown's unhappy tenure as Prime Minister, but they are not for now. For us, the most important lesson is: *take off the microphone before you get in the car.*

RADIO AND TV PHONE-INS

Politicians are expected to take calls on air from members of the public. Some are gluttons for punishment. Nick Clegg submitted himself to a weekly show, *Call Clegg*, on LBC Radio for two years, which was courageous, but didn't do him much good.

Politicians often hate phone-ins because they are unpredictable, and members of the public do not play by the rules of interviewing which presenters usually abide by. A politician who has mastered interviews can easily be kebabbed by an ordinary member of the public.

Margaret Thatcher was famously and uncharacteristically caught off-guard during the 1983 general election when she appeared on a phone-in on BBC TV's *Nationwide*. A member of the public, Mrs Diana Gould, directly challenged Mrs Thatcher over the sinking of the Argentine cruiser the *Belgrano* during the previous year's Falklands War. Thatcher was caught out, pressed again and again by Mrs Gould, and came away from the encounter visibly riled. That was the only occasion during the 1983 general election when anyone managed to get the better of her.

US President George Bush was victim of a superb piece of spin doctoring in the 1992 Presidential elections when he appeared on *Larry King Live*. As Bush appeared to have side-stepped Larry King's and callers' questions on his involvement in the Iran–Contra scandal, a call came in from a 'Mr Stephanopoulos calling from Little Rock, Arkansas'.

The call, from Bill Clinton's communications chief, appeared as though he had phoned the public access phone numbers and got lucky. Stephanopoulos, armed with proof of Bush's involvement in arms for hostages deals, embarrassed and humiliated the President live on national TV. In reality, the call had been negotiated between the Clinton war room and the *Larry King Live* producer Tammy Haddad, and the stunt hit the front pages the next day.

If you, or your boss, is invited on to a phone-in, the best advice is to treat people respectfully, no matter how odious their views. They may be rude, but you must stay calm. Use the callers' names as another way of showing respect. Don't patronise or talk down to people. Show empathy with people's predicaments. Be prepared to push back if someone is saying something with which you disagree. The point of these shows is not to spread sweetness and light.

THE VALUE OF MEDIA TRAINING

If you are asked to appear on the radio or television for the first time, you can adopt one of two approaches. You can assume that because you're good at writing documents, chairing meetings, making PowerPoint presentations or running an organisation, giving a good broadcast interview is no different and everything will be fine. After all, the airwaves are filled with people being interviewed, every minute of the day. Just turn up, make your points, and wait for the appreciative emails and tweets to start landing.

Or you can do the right thing, which is the exact opposite of that. You can decide that appearing on radio and TV is the route to tens of thousands of people, and to do it well requires skill and practice.

That's where media training comes in. I first came across the idea of media training in 1990, when I was asked to appear on the BBC One show *Wogan*. I assumed I would just turn up and be myself. When the spin doctors at the Labour Party, whose interests I was representing, discovered this, they put me through media training. I'm glad they did.

The trainer taught me all the things we've discussed in this chapter: the important of dress and non-verbal communication (out went the jeans, in came a suit), the need to hone a message and practise it out loud, the necessity to predict the questions and practise answers, and the overriding necessity of remaining unfazed by make-up, lights, wires, microphones and monitors.

Media training consists of realistic interviews with a skilled trainer role-playing the interviewer. The interviews are recorded, played back and analysed. For the trainee, it can be excruciating see themselves on camera, and to have their appearance, voice and language picked apart. That is better than conducting a 'car crash' interview which people share on Twitter for their entertainment. In fiction, a good example is the Ben Swain interview with Jeremy Paxman in *The Thick of It*, which is available in its full horror on YouTube.

In real life – take your pick. Recent examples are Chloe Smith's interview on *Newsnight*, when, as the minister, she had to admit she hadn't been consulted on the tax changes she was being interviewed about, or the shadow City minister Richard Burgon, who admitted, after a month in the job, he had not met anyone who worked in the City, and didn't know what the UK deficit for 2015 was.

Media training allows you to test your lines to destruction, to make mistakes, to demystify the programme-making process and to give your confidence a boost.

Chapter Eight

How to Do
Advanced Spinning

Journalism is often simply the industrialisation of gossip.

—ANDREW MARR

The media are obsessed with spin doctors and with portraying them as a bad thing, yet seem addicted to our medicine.

—ALASTAIR CAMPBELL

ALL SPIN DOCTORS have their own styles and favoured techniques. There are some who think it's all about menace. Others, more wisely, recognise it is all about a professional, grown-up approach to dealing with the media. A good relationship with a journalist might mean a fairer hearing, some slack, or even the willingness to 'do a deal' over a story to make it disappear. This usually means spiking an unfavourable story in return for a better story or opportunity.

There are times when special measures are needed. These are some of the things spin doctors sometimes have to do.

HOW TO HANDLE A CRISIS

If your reputation is being seriously threatened, it may be considered a crisis. A crisis situation requires a calm head, clear thought and swift action. Grown-up organisations have crisis plans, comprising a crisis team, lists of contact numbers, pre-prepared statements, and plans for 'business continuity' in the event of fire, earthquake, flood or bombs.

The spin doctor may be the canary in the coal mine. They will be the first to take a call from a Sunday newspaper that their boss is about to be exposed. They need to phone it in straight away, ascertain the facts and prepare a defence (or a resignation statement). You may discover the Sunday newspaper journalist is merely fishing and has no hard evidence. A simple denial is enough, and you breathe a sigh of relief.

Social media is essential in a crisis. This is when you need to have a senior person in charge of the Twitter and Facebook accounts, not the intern. Never leave a vacuum for others to fill. Make a statement straight away, taking the situation seriously, expressing human emotions such as empathy, and keep updating the information as you get it.

If you behave professionally, keep journalists informed and included, be honest, show compassion and empathy, and keep making your case, you may live to fight another day.

HOW TO COMPLAIN

If you feel the coverage you have received in the media is unfair or inaccurate, you should complain. The function of social media, as we have seen, is often to spread lies and distortions like wildfire. Gone are the days when you could just 'let it go' and console yourself that a damaging newspaper story is 'tomorrow's fish and chip wrapper'. Today, a damaging story is available for the rest of time.

Everyone has the right to complain if they feel they have been misrepresented or unfairly treated. Complaining is a terribly un-British thing to do, and we don't like doing it, but journalists can be guilty of terrible acts of unfairness and misrepresentation and they shouldn't be allowed to get away with it. Complaining about shoddy journalism is a public service.

Spin doctors in the political world spend a great deal of

time complaining to news organisations about the coverage they receive.

For example, back in December 1997, the *Today* programme leaked a letter from Labour's David Hill to the editor of the programme, Jon Barton. Hill, then the party's chief media spokesman, had written to complain about an especially tough John Humphrys grilling of Harriet Harman. The story appeared on the front page of *The Guardian* (13 December 1997) with a full colour picture of Humphrys under the headline 'The man Labour wants to gag'. Hill's letter is worth quoting:

> Dear John [sic],
>
> The John Humphrys problem has assumed new proportions after this morning's interview with Harriet Harman. In response, we have had a council of war and are now considering whether, as a party, we will suspend cooperation when you make bids through us for government Ministers.
>
> Individual government departments will continue to make their own minds up, but we will now give very careful thought to any bid to us, in order to make sure that your listeners are not going to be subjected to a repeat of the ridiculous exchange this morning... John Humphrys interrupted so much that she [Harman] was never permitted to develop a single answer. No one seeking to the find the Secretary of State's explanation would be any the wiser at the end of the 'interview'. Frankly, none of us feels that this can go on.

The leaked letter is an example of the process which takes place day in, day out. Complaining to editors, journalists, even owners, is part of the job. The leaked letter shows that spin doctors, as a last resort, can simply withdraw support from the news creation process, pick up their ball, and go home.

In January 2016, Jeremy Corbyn's spin doctor launched an official complaint to the BBC, accusing it of colluding with the MP Stephen Doughty to secure his resignation from the Labour front bench live on the BBC. It turned out there was no collusion, just some sharp-witted journalism by the BBC's Laura Kuenssberg.

The BBC's editor of live political programmes, Robbie Gibb, responded with a letter which batted away Labour's objections without much effort. The legacy is a soured relationship, and a million tweets from Corbynistas complaining that the BBC is part of the media conspiracy against Corbyn.

The art of complaining is knowing when to make a formal, public complaint, with hard evidence, when to write an email to show you're paying attention, and when simply to have a quiet word in the editor's ear.

The skill of the spin doctor is in knowing who to complain to: when to chastise the journalist responsible, and when to take it to their boss. In his incarnation as Labour's head of communications, Peter Mandelson's fearsome reputation stemmed from his understanding of the news creation process and his knowledge of the individual journalists working in a particular newsroom on a particular day.

If a story is incorrect, you should first of all phone the journalist responsible and point out the facts. If the journalist seems uninterested or hostile, phone up the duty editor.

(Don't threaten to go to the editor of The Times or the chairman of the BBC governors – you'll look silly.)

If the dispute is over a matter of pure accuracy such as the wrong name put under a photograph or incorrect figures, the newspaper has a duty to print a correction in the next edition. This will appear as a small paragraph at the bottom of a column, usually titled 'Correction'.

The Sun was forced by an IPSO ruling to print a correction to a story suggesting that Jeremy Corbyn would join the Privy Council in order to secure state funding for the Labour Party. There was no link. The Sun's retraction appeared on page one, but comprised eleven words in a box 15mm by 35mm.

If your complaint rests on being misquoted, things are less simple. Journalists have the right to use part of what you say, to paraphrase what you say, and to put words into your mouth by asking you to agree with statements they put to you. If your quote is made up, or gives a meaning entirely different from what you actually meant, you have grounds to complain.

If your complaint is non-factual, and based on a sense of unfairness or distortion, you are on shakier ground, but you should still complain. You might appeal to a sense of fair play and natural justice, or to the news organisation's own producer guidelines, code of conduct, or even the National Union of Journalists (NUJ) code of conduct. This includes the stipulations that 'a journalist shall strive to ensure that the information he/she disseminates is fair and accurate, avoids the expression of comment and conjecture as established fact', and that 'a journalist shall rectify promptly any harmful inaccuracies, ensure that correction and apologies receive due prominence and afford the right to reply to persons criticised when the issue is of sufficient importance'.

Following the phone call, you should write a letter (marked 'not for publication') setting out your complaints. Marshal your case clearly and use rock solid facts. Copy the letter to the editor or producer.

Because all news is online and rolling, and updated minute by minute, you can shape a story by complaining about it, by introducing new facts or mitigating factors, and by showing that you're keeping an eye on what the journalist is doing. Most will not knowingly publish something which is simply inaccurate.

If you cannot get redress through the informal route, you can escalate it to an official complaint to the press watchdog IPSO (the Independent Press Standards Organisation), which was set up to replace the Press Complaints Commission (PCC) following the Leveson Inquiry into phone-hacking. The IPSO website takes you through how to do it, and on what grounds you can make complaints. The website also helpfully publishes complaints and their outcome, so you can judge what might work for you. The IPSO Editors' Code of Practice is reproduced at the back of this book, so you can see the standard that the newspapers and magazines have set themselves. It is worth noting that The Guardian, Financial Times and Observer have not signed up to IPSO, and have their own complaints procedures.

RAPID REBUTTAL

Rapid rebuttal is the technique used in political campaigns when spin doctors are engaged in hand-to-hand combat. It rests on the idea that no claim by the opposition should be allowed to be accepted as the truth. This is especially true online, where a lie about you can be spread across social media in a few seconds. That's why you need to invest time in monitoring social media, using a system such as Hootsuite, to know what people are saying about you.

In Labour's pre-Mandelson days, the party would allow the Tories to tell all kinds of lies, and do nothing about it. The rationale was that by responding, it gave them a dignity they didn't deserve, and that people wouldn't believe the nonsense put out by Conservative Central Office. Unfortunately, the strategy was flawed, because people did believe the nonsense, and if you throw enough mud, some of it sticks.

By the 1997 general election, senior Tories couldn't sneeze without Labour putting out a rebuttal. It was an awesome process to watch. No Tory speech, news conference or news release went unchecked. Within hours, sometimes within minutes, journalists would have something in their hands from Labour, putting their side of the argument, disputing the Tories' facts and pointing out inconsistencies.

Labour's impressive rapid rebuttal was based on a computer database system called Excalibur (Excalibur was the sword of truth in Arthurian legend), which logged thousands of articles, speeches and news releases. If a Tory candidate said something on pensions, Labour's spin doctors had access within minutes to everything that person had ever said in public on pensions. It all sounds a little old-fashioned, but at the time it was highly effective.

Of course, any database is only as good as the people using it. Many of the successes of Labour's rapid rebuttal were because of the humans operating the system, not the computer itself.

The lesson of Labour's rapid rebuttal operation for spin doctors everywhere is that nothing said by your opponents and rivals should ever be allowed to go unchallenged without your own version of the truth being available. If a lie or distortion is allowed to be accepted, then people may assume it is true, no matter how absurd.

If someone else is shaping opinion about you on Facebook or Twitter, then you have lost control. Some of the lies that Labour failed to tackle in the early '80s (for example, that Labour councils banned black bin liners and the nursery rhyme 'Baa Baa Black Sheep') are still believed by some people. The lies have become accepted as fact.

NEWS CONFERENCES

News conferences are usually more trouble than they're worth. The first question to ask is: is the story important enough to warrant a news conference? If the story is major – a new premier league football signing, a resignation from the Cabinet, a new panellist on *The Voice*, then you just need to tweet it, and stand back and watch it grow.

If you are announcing the winner of the local darts league or a change of venue for the retired men's club monthly meeting, forget it. Those spin doctors working in-house, or as consultants, often face the pressure from employers or clients who fancy the idea of jostling journalists thrusting mics into their faces and flashbulbs flashing. Such pressures must be resisted, because there are few situations more embarrassing than an empty news conference. It is the stuff of spin doctors' nightmares.

If you are absolutely sure that you want to run a news conference, then it needs to be meticulously planned.

First, choose your venue wisely. To entice journalists away from their desks, it must be convenient for them. A story about rural poverty among crofters in the Highlands will not receive much coverage if the news conference is held in a rural crofter's cottage up a mountain. A group of crofters staging a press conference in central Edinburgh or London have a much better chance. The mountain has to come to Mohammed.

So pick a central location near the news centre in your town and region. You can choose a venue because it contains a subtle connotation. When Alastair Campbell was defending himself to the media after the Hutton Inquiry in 2004, he chose the traditional surroundings of the Foreign Press Association in London. He made his statements from the bottom of a sweeping staircase in a building which had once been home to Gladstone. He wanted to reinforce the image of respectability. Some venues imply solid dependability (hotels, institutes, libraries) and others create the impression of innovation (the Institute for Contemporary Art in London, or the Life Centre in Newcastle).

Choose a room large enough to accommodate the expected number of journalists, but not so large that it looks empty even with twenty hacks. If you expect television crews, ensure that there is space near the front for them to set up their equipment, and lots of plug sockets.

Make sure there is a backdrop with your organisational logo and name. The top table should be covered, and uncluttered by cups of coffee and newspapers. It is usually the spin doctor's job to pay attention to detail.

The line-up for press conferences can be a matter of great controversy, as everyone wants the limelight. But the spin doctor must be disciplined and keep the top table from looking like a police identity parade. Make sure it's not all men.

The best approach is a chair to introduce the speakers, the lead spokesman for the organisation (the chief executive) to provide the corporate line, and an expert (head of research, the author of the report being launched) to provide factual information as a backup.

Have a hashtag for Twitter, and film it yourself for use on your own sites and YouTube channel.

HOW TO LEAK

Leaking is the process of giving a journalist information which is not officially sanctioned for release. A leak is a well-practised device, designed to promote a cause or steer a public argument.

Sometimes they are used to 'fly kites'; that is to test an idea with the public, but also to be able to deny it. Often, they are used to undermine an opponent. Leaking might involve passing documents over to a journalist, or 'leaving them on the photocopier' to be found.

Leaks might be the product of heroic whistle-blowers wanting to right some injustice, but mostly they are from spin doctors trying to manipulate events. Everyone is at it, even Prime Ministers. The Ship of State, it is often said, is the only ship which leaks from the top.

There is a standard-issue joke about leaking information to journalists, that leaking is an irregular verb: I brief, you leak, he or she spills their guts. The morality rests on how successful it is, and whether history judges the act kindly.

Few dispute the value of Desmond Morton, a civil servant, leaking details of German aircraft production to Winston Churchill, then a backbencher, in order to build the case against appeasement of Hitler.

On the other hand, leaks from the Cabinet in 2012, when Chris Huhne had a row with George Osborne about the conduct of the referendum on changes to the electoral system, were hardly in the public interest.

Damian McBride's memoir *Power Trip* contains a catalogue of leaks, strongly suggesting the leaker was doing so for the thrill of it and to seek the favour of journalists, rather than for any strategic goal. These included his weekly effort to discover the background to departmental announcements listed on the communications 'grid' and to then rewrite them and hand them over to journalists.

If a spin doctor is to leak information to a journalist, it should be done under licence, and not as part of some freelance activity. A judicious leak can be used to help win an argument or stop something daft happening. In January 2016, Margaret Beckett issued her report on the reasons why Labour did not win the 2015 general election. Many felt she had pulled her punches.

Some days later, another report, based on focus groups conducted by pollster Deborah Mattinson, appeared in the media. It was much tougher and apportioned blame more clearly. The report had not been published, but somehow appeared in the clutches of Robert Peston at ITN.

The most important thing about leaking is that you don't get found out. There can be no 'fingerprints' at the scene of the crime. So you need to be careful not to leak anything which only you, or a small circle, have access to. You can't make it look too obvious. If you can, you should leak something, but make it look like someone else has leaked it. This might lead to the double advantage of getting the information out, and blaming someone else at the same time.

HOW TO BRIEF AGAINST YOUR ENEMIES

When things turn nasty, spin doctors have to brief the media against their enemies. (Enemies should never be confused with opponents. Your opponents are those in rival firms, teams, organisations or parties who are just doing their job in trying to get you. Enemies are the ones who often claim to be your friends. Your enemies are usually 'within'.)

The established spin doctor can use his or her trusted relationship with a journalist to do their enemy down: so-and-so is destined for the chop, so-and-so is weak and spineless.

Damian McBride's *Power Trip* recounts endless briefings, or accusations of briefings by McBride against 'Blairite' ministers, or the likes of Ed Miliband and Douglas Alexander. It reveals a murky world of briefing and counter-briefing, blame and recrimination and ultimately broken relationships between colleagues. Ed Miliband, believing, wrongly, McBride to be the source of briefing against him, broke his friendship with him.

It was spin doctors, using the unattributable briefing as cover, who described union boss Bill Morris in a newspaper as 'pusillanimous', who described John Biffen as a 'semi-detached member of the government', and who called Gordon Brown 'psychologically flawed', a claim which was splashed by *The Observer* on 18 January 1998 and which sparked a new phase of warfare between the Brown and Blair camps.

Fast forward to January 2016, and Labour spin doctors are still at it. Michael Dugher MP, sacked from the front bench by

Jeremy Corbyn, wrote that 'there was this barrage of briefing saying that good, decent, loyal members of the shadow Cabinet – named at length – would be fired in a "revenge reshuffle" because they took a different position to Jeremy on a free vote on Syria'. The Corbyn camp then sought revenge in the reshuffle by sacking Dugher, and briefing against him to newspapers. Their attack line, that he was 'incompetent', rang a little hollow, given their incompetence in handing the media during the reshuffle. This point was made by Dugher on Twitter.

My advice to those considering briefing against people is: *don't*. No good will come of it. But if you want to ignore my advice, make sure it's business, not personal; use material which is true, not lies; never involve someone's family; and remember Jesus' words that those who take up the sword shall perish by the sword. And for heaven's sake, don't get caught doing it. If possible, make it look like it came from someone else. Create a 'false flag' so that the finger of blame points elsewhere.

MISINFORMATION

This really belongs to the world of espionage and conspiracy theory, rather than spin doctoring. The spin doctor is finished if caught deliberately lying to journalists. You can tell some of the truth, even leave information out of the discussion, but to tell a straightforward lie is professional suicide. Black propaganda is the stuff of the KGB, CIA and MI5.

That's not to say you can't have some fun. Alastair
Campbell persuaded us that John Major tucked his shirt into
his underpants.

Perhaps the most famous example of misinformation is the
Zinoviev letter. The Zinoviev letter was the invitation (probably
forged by the British Secret Service) in 1924 from the Soviet
leadership to the British working class to start the revolution.
It appeared on the front pages of the right-wing newspapers
in the week of the August 1924 general election, and undoubt-
edly cost the Labour Party votes.

The reds-under-the-beds scare story was still working even
after the fall of communism. In the 1992 general election, the
Sunday Times ran a front-page story claiming to have unearthed
'Kinnock's Kremlin Connection'. The 'connection' rested on
the discovery of a KGB file on Kinnock – no great surprise, as the
KGB had files on all the leaders in western democracies,
including Margaret Thatcher and Ronald Reagan.

Peter Wright's revelations in Spycatcher showed that a group
of intelligence officers sought to malign politicians by starting rumours and spreading misinformation with journalists.
This included the ludicrous suggestion that Harold Wilson and
Edward Heath were Soviet agents, various government ministers were communists, and that Labour leader Hugh Gaitskell
was murdered by the KGB. In the lead-up to the February 1974
general election, Peter Wright claims that:

MI5 would arrange for selective details of the intelligence about
leading Labour Party figures, but especially Wilson, to be leaked to

sympathetic pressmen. Using our contacts in the press and among union officials, word of the material contained in the MI5 files and the fact that Wilson was considered a security risk would be passed around.

Journalist Paul Foot claimed that during the 1970s, journalists often took phone calls from 'freelance journalists' offering photographic evidence of Conservative leader Edward Heath's over-familiarity with young male Swedes, or similar. The photos didn't exist, but the gossip would soon spread through the pubs and wine bars of Fleet Street and Westminster.

These days, 'smear' has become a much overused word. Keyboard warriors seem to think it means anything written about Jeremy Corbyn they don't like, including verifiable reports of his actual views and statements.

There are any number of malicious rumours doing the rounds about senior figures at any given moment: so-and-so hits his wife, so-and-so is sleeping with his secretary, so-and-so is secretly gay, so-and-so has a drink problem, and on it goes. The internet provides fertile ground for these rumours to fester. Certain political sites anchor their business on them. No one, not even important and powerful people, can be having that much fun for all the rumours to be true.

HOW TO CHANGE THE NARRATIVE

Spin doctors need to be able to redirect the media narrative, and send it in a different direction. In politics, this moment comes when the other side are starting to gain positive coverage and get 'traction' for their point of view. The way to do this is to start a new conversation about something else, preferably something more eye-catching and engaging.

Let's see how Boris Johnson explained it in The Spectator in March 2013:

> Let us suppose you are losing an argument. The facts are overwhelmingly against you, and the more people focus on the reality the worse it is for you and your case. Your best bet in these circumstances is to perform a manoeuvre that a great campaigner describes as 'throwing a dead cat on the table, mate'.
>
> That is because there is one thing that is absolutely certain about throwing a dead cat on the dining room table – and I don't mean that people will be outraged, alarmed, disgusted. That is true, but irrelevant. The key point, says my Australian friend, is that everyone will shout 'Jeez, mate, there's a dead cat on the table!'; in other words they will be talking about the dead cat, the thing you want them to talk about, and they will not be talking about the issue that has been causing you so much grief.

And there it is: the famous Dead Cat strategy, advocated by Australian campaign guru Lynton Crosby, the so-called Wizard of Oz. An example was when Tory minister Michael Fallon raised the issue of Ed Miliband 'stabbing his brother in the back' to become Labour leader, during the 2015 general election. The line ran that Miliband was unfit for high office. Many commentators were outraged at the personal attack, and wrote their columns to say so. This merely served to highlight the dead cat on the table.

HOW TO RUN A SPOILER

Spoiler means different things to different people. Most people these days would define it as giving away a detail from the plot of a film or book which spoils another person's enjoyment of it. (For example, Bruce Willis is a ghost who befriends a little boy.) A review of a film or book might include a 'spoiler alert' to warn the reader in advance.

In journalism, a spoiler is when one media outlet nicks a story off their rival and runs it first. But in spin doctoring, a spoiler is when you deliberately give a story to other journalists to undermine the journalist with the exclusive. It's a method of diluting the impact of a negative exclusive. Also, if you spread the story around, it might come and go in one news cycle, whereas if it appears as a big story in the *Mail on Sunday*, it will guarantee a 'day two' story in the rest of the papers on Monday.

As previously mentioned, in the fevered run-up to the 1992 general election, the *Sunday Times* unearthed some nonsense about then-Labour Leader Neil Kinnock being on KGB files. (The implication being that he must somehow be a Soviet 'agent of influence'). As soon as David Hill, Labour's spin doctor-in-chief, was tipped off about the *Sunday Times*'s intentions to run the spurious 'exclusive' as a front-page lead, 'Kinnock's

Kremlin Connection', he didn't try and persuade them to stop it. He engaged in the spoiler: he spent his Saturday night phoning all the *Sunday Times*'s rival papers and giving them the story. Thus he destroyed the *Sunday Times*'s hopes of an exclusive and the impact of the story, and ensured that the other papers carried the story with plenty of Labour spin.

In 2005, Michael Crick was researching his biography of the Conservative Party leader, Michael Howard. His research led him to believe that Howard's grandfather was an 'illegal immigrant', which, given the Conservative Party's tough line on immigration, made for a great story. Crick approached Guy Black, then the opposition leader's press spokesperson, for verification of the story. Instead of coming back to Crick, Howard's office gave the story to the *Daily Mail* as a spoiler.

BRIBERY

Can journalists be bribed? In many cultures, it is normal for spin doctors to pay for journalists' 'expenses' in order to get them to cover a story. Many of the people I've met from parts of Africa tell me paying journalists to cover stories is perfectly normal. In Nigeria, for example, an organisation will pay journalists 'expenses' to cover a story, which in effect is a payment to give the story a positive spin.

In the UK, journalists cannot be bribed. That's not to say they don't appreciate a good lunch at the Ivy or a day at Lord's or Wimbledon. Spin doctors can arrange trips and visits, access to celebrity-laden events and goody bags of free stuff. Is this bribery?

There is a growing and unethical form of bribery in journalism which involves linking the publication of editorial material to the placing of advertisements. In other words, unscrupulous publications will use your story, as long as your organisation pays for an advert in the same publication. The coverage is conditional on the payment. This tends to be practised by smaller magazines and local papers.

However, rest assured that large-scale bribery plays no part in spin doctoring. The spin doctor need never resort to such obvious and disreputable tactics, because, as the famous words of Humbert Wolfe rightly tell us:

You cannot hope to bribe or twist,
thank God! the British journalist.
But, seeing what the man will do
unbribed, there's no occasion to.

Conclusion

Into the Light

*The art of publicity is a black art; but it has come
to stay, and every year adds to its potency.*

—Thomas Paine

W E ARE NO more likely to witness the end of
spin doctoring than we are to witness the
end of rain or sunshine. For as long as there
are newspapers, radio and television, and
the internet, then there will be people who try to influence
what they print and broadcast.

In August 1996, Clare Short MP described the political
spin doctors as 'people who live in the dark'. Since the 1990s,

political spinners have been dragged from the dark into the media spotlight. This is no bad thing. It's not that long since the existence of a Prime Minister's spokesperson was officially denied. The same is true for spinners across the sectors: it is time to take off their masks.

The more transparent and open the process of news creation becomes, the better it is for democracy. The more clearly we understand where the news we read, watch and listen to has come from, the better informed we will become.

In the future, I hope that no one reads a newspaper or tweet or watches a news bulletin in a state of passive receptiveness. The news and views presented by our social media, newspapers, radio and television should be treated with the same healthy scepticism that we currently reserve for advertising.

All citizens should understand that news comes from certain processes, and is not doled out as a result of unseen forces or magic. We should be querulous and questioning, and not accept with naive trust what journalists tell us.

The power that social media gives us is allowing us to bypass the traditional bastions of media power; we can create our own content; we can shape opinions and forge reputations. It is an awesome responsibility, with which many people are still grappling, like a child with a box of matches.

The more people can influence the media, can make themselves heard, can complain when things go wrong, and can stop journalists misrepresenting them, the better media we will have. The better the media, the more open and vibrant our society becomes.

Glossary of Spin Doctoring Terms

I F YOU WANT to sound like you know what you're talking about, you need to know some of the lingo used in the worlds of journalism and public relations. Here are some terms you'll need on your adventures in spin:

ABC: the Audit Bureau of Circulation is the place to go to find out how many people are buying a publication, and who they are.

Above the fold: this is literally the top half of a newspaper, and therefore the prominent part of the page for a story to appear. As a spin doctor, you get extra marks for placing a story 'above the fold'. Also it applies to websites – the bit you can read onscreen without scrolling down.

Advertorial: a blend of advertising and editorial, blurring the divide between paid-for and non-paid-for content.

Angle: the aspect of a story which you choose to stress, usually one of the **five Ws (q.v.)**. Also known as 'peg' (the thing on which the story hangs).

Aston: the description that appears on the TV screen under the name of a spokesperson or interviewee, designed to let viewers know who they are. e.g. 'Prime Minister', 'Church of England' or 'anti-fracking campaigner'. Named after the Aston machine which makes the words appear.

Background: part of an article which supplies information to place the story in context. Also, information supplied by a spin doctor to a journalist to place a story in context.

Broadsheet: big-format newspaper such as *The Times* or *Telegraph*. These days, 'broadsheet' refers more to the content being serious-minded than the actual size.

By-line: the name of the journalist who has written the piece, which appears above their article. If accompanied by a picture of them, it's a **photo by-line**. The by-line 'By Our Correspondent' often means the **copy (q.v.)** has come from a news agency. Sometimes, several journalists' names appear in the by-line to obscure the source for the story.

Cans: jargon for headphones in radio stations.

Case study: what journalists love – 'real people'. A case study is an example of a person or group of people describing their experiences, and available for journalists to use.

Churnalism: a neologism for sloppy journalism which just churns out other people's material, such as news statements.

Clip: a short piece of sound recorded for radio, or a short **sound bite (q.v.)** for TV.

Columnist: a journalist who writes a column with their opinions and views on events. The big-hitters form the **commentariat**.

Commission: this is when a publication asks someone to write a piece.

Conference: the morning meeting of newsroom staff on a publication or broadcaster to discuss stories for that day's running order or edition of daily newspaper.

Contact: person with useful information or services. For the spin doctor, the most useful contacts tend to be journalists (although not necessarily vice versa).

Copy: the words written by a journalist (hopefully to deadline).

Copy flow: the route which **copy (q.v.)** takes within a news organisation, usually from reporter to **sub (q.v.)** to section editor to editor. A good spin doctor understands the copy flow within an organisation, in order to be able to have influence at different levels.

Cover lines: the words on the front of a magazine or newspaper enticing you inside.

Crop: to cut a photograph to make it fit the space in a publication, or to create a particular effect.

Crosshead: a small heading used to break up a column of text, usually centred.

Cub: a trainee reporter, usually impoverished.

Cuttings/cuts: this used to be the files of articles sliced from newspapers. Hence an autobiography which relies on published articles rather than fresh sources can be dismissed as a 'cuttings job'.

Deadline: the time the article is due. For journalists, they are unmissable, so the deadline they give the spin doctor for a comment or response will be longer than the real deadline. For writers, deadlines are more flexible, hence the great quote by Douglas Adams: 'I love *deadlines*. I love the whooshing noise they make as they go by.'

Diary: humorous, gossipy, trivial column appearing in most newspapers and magazines, filled with tales of the embarrassments and misdemeanours of the great and the good. Usually appears under a *nom de plume*, although written by a team of writers. Under threat from faster outfits such as the Guido Fawkes website.

Down-spin: to play down the importance of a (usually damaging) event or statement. 'That's not important; this really isn't a story...' See **up-spin**.

DPS: a double-page spread. Content, usually **copy (q.v.)**, graphics and pictures, across two pages, which means more prominence for the subject matter.

Editorial: the column in a newspaper which expresses its own opinion on a matter of importance. Also: all **copy (q.v.)** in a newspaper that is not advertising material.

Embargo: the time stipulated on a news release before which information cannot be published (but can be acted upon).

Exclusive: story given to one news outlet to the exclusion of all the others. Useful tool of spin doctoring, as this creates leverage over how the story is run, and earns credits in the bank with the journalist you give it to. Can annoy all the others.

Feature: longer article (as distinct from news) which covers an issue in greater depth, with more detail and colour, and less constrained by the conventions of news reporting.

Filler: a short article used to fill up space in a publication. The spoof trivial **columnist (q.v.)** in *Private Eye* is called Polly Filler.

Five Ws: the components of a story: who, what, where, why and when.

Flatplan: a plan of a publication to show how the **copy (q.v.)**, images and adverts will look on the pages.

Freebie: the free stuff, often contained in **goody bags**, which publicity departments give out to journalists covering a new movie, car, phone, etc.

Ghost-writer: one employed to write articles, letters, even books in the name of another person. Articles in tabloid newspapers 'by the Prime Minister' are a safe bet as examples of ghost-writing.

Green room: the hospitality suite where TV outfits sometimes offer their interview guests food and drink before going on air.

Hack: jocular and mildly derisory word for journalist. Also slang for a student political activist.

Headline: the words at the top of the article designed by **subs (q.v.)** to get you to read on.

Kill fee: this is the paltry sum a freelance might receive if the article they've been **commissioned (q.v.)** to write is 'spiked' at the last minute.

Lead time: the length of time ahead of publication that a journalist works on their articles. On a big glossy magazine, it could be six months; on a website ten minutes.

Leak: the unauthorised release of confidential material to the media. (Or the pretence of doing so, orchestrated by a spin doctor.)

Leveson Inquiry or 'Leveson': the government inquiry into journalistic ethics, launched after the phone-hacking scandal. Led to the creation of the Independent Press Standards Organisation (IPSO) and the demise of the Press Complaints Commission (PCC).

NCTJ: The National Council for the Training of Journalists. Most working journalists have an NCTJ qualification under their belts.

News: what every journalist wants to cover.

News agency: news-gathering organisation which sells its news and information to print and broadcast media.

Local, national and international agencies (e.g. Press Association, Reuters) serve newsrooms via an online link-up, still known as a **'wire' (q.v.)**. (As in: 'What's running on the wires?')

News conference: an event where journalists are given information from an organisation or individual. Usually only used for high-profile news stories.

News desk: the front line in a news operation, where news, information and tip-offs are first received by reporters, and news stories are written.

News release: the short document emailed to journalists by spin doctors to entice them into covering your story. Most news releases end up in the bin within seconds of receipt. As well as news, they can cover operational information and notice of events like **news conferences (q.v.)** and **photo opportunities (q.v.)**.

NIB: 'news in brief'. This can be a standalone, short, sharp news story of fifty to 100 words.

NUJ: the National Union of Journalists.

On spec: when you send an article to the media without prior agreement for publication, in the hope that it will be used (although the chances are it won't).

On the record/Off the record: convention which allows you to plant information without any fingerprints, but can be easily ignored by journalists.

Op ed: the page in a newspaper opposite the **editorial (q.v.)**, usually used for longer **think pieces (q.v.)** and opinion features.

Package: a broadcast report made of different components: interview, comment or music.

Panel: the sections of text pulled out of an article (usually attention-grabbing phrases) and placed between two lines, used to break up long articles.

Par: journalists' shorthand for paragraph. Sometimes **para.**

Patch: the geographical area covered by a local newspaper, or the area covered by a particular journalist.

Photo opportunity: an event staged to provide newspapers with good photographs, which also contain messages from the organisation.

Pre-recorded: the term denoting that a radio or television interview is taped in advance of broadcast, and can be subject to editing.

Press officer: Old-fashioned term for **PRO (q.v.)**.

Press release: see **news release.**

PRO: Public relations officer (or 'press relations officer'). This is a junior spin doctor employed by an organisation to draft and issue **news releases (q.v.)**, field calls from journalists, write articles, monitor social media and run the Twitter account.

Puff: over-the-top sucking-up to an editor, client, product manufacturer or your boss in an article or news release. Also: **puffery, puff piece.**

Screamer: newspaper slang for exclamation mark.

Script: a broadcaster's lines.

Silly season: the period each year around August when most people are on holiday, and therefore there's little hard news. This can be the spin doctor's most fruitful time, because newsrooms are desperate for material. Usually, the silly season is when stories appear about crop circles, Elvis sightings, shock survey results and unfounded speculation about political plots.

Sound bite: the short, snappy phrase used to make a point on radio or TV, usually under fifteen seconds long. E.g. 'Tough on crime, tough on the causes of crime'.

Source: the person telling journalists something, protected by the journalists' code of omerta. Journalists go to jail rather than reveal a source.

Spin control: the influence on the process of news creation exercised by spin doctors.

Spin doctor: if you don't know by now...

Splash: the lead story on the front page of a newspaper.

Spoiler: a story which appears before a rival's, thus spoiling theirs.

Standfirst: the text between the **headline (q.v.)** and the main text, often used on **features (q.v.)** and longer news pieces, to draw the reader into the article.

Style guide: the organisation's guide to all things relating to spelling, punctuation, grammar and format: **the house style**. Designed to ensure consistency across the publication or organisation.

Sub-editor (sub): print journalist who checks and edits spelling, grammar and house style, writes **headlines (q.v.)**, captions for photographs, **panels (q.v.)** and **standfirsts (q.v.)**, lays out the page and cuts articles (and journalists) down to size. The sub-editor in charge is called the 'chief sub' and the sub-editor charged with giving the page a final check is the 'stone sub'. The rest of the sub-editors are called 'down-table subs'.

Tabloid: in the UK, these are the 'red tops' such as *The Sun* and *Mirror*. Loud, brash, funny, filthy, with huge circulations.

Target audience: the people the spin doctor wants to reach. This audience might be huge, such as all ABC1s, or it might be a small group of opinion formers.

Think piece: contemplative, longer article tackling a thorny subject. So called because the piece is designed to make you think.

Up-spin: to use phrases which accentuate the importance of a seemingly unimportant event or statement.

Vox pop: 'voice of the people' interview with members of the public, usually conducted in the street on a particular subject.

Wire: a **news agency (q.v.)** (Press Association, Reuters or Associated Press) which pumps stories and photographs straight into newsrooms.

WOB: 'white out of black'. Term used to describe a **headline (q.v.)** reversed out of a black background, for extra visual emphasis.

Word count: the number of words required for a piece. As a spin doctor, you may be asked for three or four **pars (q.v.)** for a piece, or 500 words for a website. Never go over, or under, the word count.

Appendix

The Editors' Code of Practice

THE INDEPENDENT PRESS Standards Organisation (IPSO), as regulator, is charged with enforcing the following Code of Practice, which was framed by the Editors' Code of Practice Committee and is enshrined in the contractual agreement between IPSO and newspaper, magazine and electronic news publishers.

PREAMBLE

The Code – including this preamble and the public interest exceptions below – sets the framework for the highest

professional standards that members of the press subscrib-
ing to the Independent Press Standards Organisation have
undertaken to maintain. It is the cornerstone of the system
of voluntary self-regulation to which they have made a bind-
ing contractual commitment. It balances both the rights of
the individual and the public's right to know.

To achieve that balance, it is essential that an agreed Code
be honoured not only to the letter, but in the full spirit. It
should be interpreted neither so narrowly as to compromise
its commitment to respect the rights of the individual, nor so
broadly that it infringes the fundamental right to freedom of
expression – such as to inform, to be partisan, to challenge,
to shock, to be satirical and to entertain – or prevents publication in the public interest.

It is the responsibility of editors and publishers to apply
the Code to editorial material in both printed and online versions of their publications. They should take care to ensure it
is observed rigorously by all editorial staff and external contributors, including non-journalists.

Editors must maintain in-house procedures to resolve complaints swiftly and, where required to do so, cooperate with
IPSO. A publication subject to an adverse adjudication must
publish it in full and with due prominence, as required by IPSO.

1. Accuracy

  i)   The Press must take care not to publish inaccurate,
       misleading or distorted information or images,
       including headlines not supported by the text.

ii) A significant inaccuracy, misleading statement or distortion must be corrected, promptly and with due prominence, and – where appropriate – an apology published. In cases involving IPSO, due prominence should be as required by the regulator.

iii) A fair opportunity to reply to significant inaccuracies should be given, when reasonably called for.

iv) The Press, while free to editorialise and campaign, must distinguish clearly between comment, conjecture and fact.

v) A publication must report fairly and accurately the outcome of an action for defamation to which it has been a party, unless an agreed settlement states otherwise, or an agreed statement is published.

2. *Privacy

i) Everyone is entitled to respect for his or her private and family life, home, health and correspondence, including digital communications.

ii) Editors will be expected to justify intrusions into any individual's private life without consent. Account will be taken of the complainant's own public disclosures of information.

iii) It is unacceptable to photograph individuals, without their consent, in public or private places where there is a reasonable expectation of privacy.

3. *Harassment

i) Journalists must not engage in intimidation, harassment or persistent pursuit.

ii) They must not persist in questioning, telephoning, pursuing or photographing individuals once asked to desist; nor remain on property when asked to leave and must not follow them. If requested, they must identify themselves and whom they represent.

iii) Editors must ensure these principles are observed by those working for them and take care not to use non-compliant material from other sources.

4. Intrusion into grief or shock

In cases involving personal grief or shock, enquiries and approaches must be made with sympathy and discretion and publication handled sensitively. These provisions should not restrict the right to report legal proceedings.

5. *Reporting suicide

When reporting suicide, to prevent simulative acts care should be taken to avoid excessive detail of the method used, while taking into account the media's right to report legal proceedings.

6. *Children

i) All pupils should be free to complete their time at school without unnecessary intrusion.

ii) They must not be approached or photographed at school without permission of the school authorities.

iii) Children under sixteen must not be interviewed or photographed on issues involving their own or another child's welfare unless a custodial parent or similarly responsible adult consents.

iv) Children under sixteen must not be paid for material involving their welfare, nor parents or guardians for material about their children or wards, unless it is clearly in the child's interest.

v) Editors must not use the fame, notoriety or position of a parent or guardian as sole justification for publishing details of a child's private life.

7. *Children in sex cases

i) The press must not, even if legally free to do so, identify children under sixteen who are victims or witnesses in cases involving sex offences.

ii) In any press report of a case involving a sexual offence against a child – a) The child must not be identified.
b) The adult may be identified. c) The word 'incest' must not be used where a child victim might be identified.
d) Care must be taken that nothing in the report implies the relationship between the accused and the child.

8. *Hospitals

i) Journalists must identify themselves and obtain permission from a responsible executive before entering non-public areas of hospitals or similar institutions to pursue enquiries.

ii) The restrictions on intruding into privacy are particularly relevant to enquiries about individuals in hospitals or similar institutions.

9. *Reporting of crime

    i) Relatives or friends of persons convicted or accused of crime should not generally be identified without their consent, unless they are genuinely relevant to the story.

    ii) Particular regard should be paid to the potentially vulnerable position of children who witness, or are victims of, crime. This should not restrict the right to report legal proceedings.

10. *Clandestine devices and subterfuge

    i) The press must not seek to obtain or publish material acquired by using hidden cameras or clandestine listening devices; or by intercepting private or mobile telephone calls, messages or emails; or by the unauthorised removal of documents or photographs; or by accessing digitally held information without consent.

    ii) Engaging in misrepresentation or subterfuge, including by agents or intermediaries, can generally be justified only in the public interest and then only when the material cannot be obtained by other means.

11. Victims of sexual assault

    The press must not identify victims of sexual assault or publish material likely to contribute to such identification unless there is adequate justification and they are legally free to do so.

12. Discrimination

    i) The press must avoid prejudicial or pejorative reference to an individual's race, colour, religion, sex, gender identity,

    sexual orientation or to any physical or mental illness
    or disability.

ii) Details of an individual's race, colour, religion, gender
identity, sexual orientation, physical or mental illness or
disability must be avoided unless genuinely relevant to
the story.

13. Financial journalism

i) Even where the law does not prohibit it, journalists must
not use for their own profit financial information they
receive in advance of its general publication, nor should
they pass such information to others.

ii) They must not write about shares or securities in whose
performance they know that they or their close families
have a significant financial interest without disclosing
the interest to the editor or financial editor.

iii) They must not buy or sell, either directly or through
nominees or agents, shares or securities about which they
have written recently or about which they intend to write
in the near future.

14. Confidential sources

Journalists have a moral obligation to protect confidential
sources of information.

15. Witness payments in criminal trials

i) No payment or offer of payment to a witness – or any
person who may reasonably be expected to be called as

a witness – should be made in any case once proceedings
are active as defined by the Contempt of Court Act 1981.
This prohibition lasts until the suspect has been freed
unconditionally by police without charge or bail or the
proceedings are otherwise discontinued; or has entered
a guilty plea to the court; or, in the event of a not guilty
plea, the court has announced its verdict.

*ii) Where proceedings are not yet active but are likely and
foreseeable, editors must not make or offer payment to
any person who may reasonably be expected to be called
as a witness, unless the information concerned ought
demonstrably to be published in the public interest
and there is an over-riding need to make or promise
payment for this to be done; and all reasonable steps
have been taken to ensure no financial dealings influence
the evidence those witnesses give. In no circumstances
should such payment be conditional on the outcome
of a trial.

*iii) Any payment or offer of payment made to a person later
cited to give evidence in proceedings must be disclosed
to the prosecution and defence. The witness must be
advised of this requirement.

16. *Payment to criminals

i)   Payment or offers of payment for stories, pictures or
information which seek to exploit a particular crime or to
glorify or glamorise crime in general, must not be made
directly or via agents to convicted or confessed criminals

or to their associates – who may include family, friends
and colleagues.

ii) Editors invoking the public interest to justify payment or
offers would need to demonstrate that there was good
reason to believe the public interest would be served.
If, despite payment, no public interest emerged, then
the material should not be published.

There may be exceptions to the clauses marked * where they
can be demonstrated to be in the public interest.

THE PUBLIC INTEREST

1. The public interest includes, but is not confined to:
    i)   Detecting or exposing crime, or the threat of crime,
         or serious impropriety.
    ii) Protecting public health or safety.
    iii) Protecting the public from being misled by an action or
         statement of an individual or organisation.
    iv) Disclosing a person or organisation's failure or likely failure
         to comply with any obligation to which they are subject.
    v)   Disclosing a miscarriage of justice.
    vi) Raising or contributing to a matter of public debate,
         including serious cases of impropriety, unethical conduct
         or incompetence concerning the public.
    vii) Disclosing concealment, or likely concealment, of any
         of the above.

2. There is a public interest in freedom of expression itself.

3. The regulator will consider the extent to which material is already in the public domain or will become so.

4. Editors invoking the public interest will need to demonstrate that they reasonably believed publication – or journalistic activity taken with a view to publication – would both serve, and be proportionate to, the public interest and explain how they reached that decision at the time.

5. An exceptional public interest would need to be demonstrated to over-ride the normally paramount interests of children under sixteen.

About the Author

FOR TWENTY-FIVE YEARS, Paul Richards has helped organisations and individuals with their communications and presentation. He runs training courses in media interviews, effective writing and dealing with the media. He has worked in Tanzania, Kenya, Ghana, South Africa, Pakistan and Iraq, and across the UK.

Paul was a special adviser to two Cabinet ministers, in three government departments, under two Labour Prime Ministers. He has also worked in the communications departments of three London local authorities and the Royal National Institute for Deaf People (RNID). He has lectured at Queen Mary, University of London (QMUL), and the School of Oriental and African Studies (SOAS).

He has appeared on *Newsnight*, the *Today* programme, Sky News, *Channel 4 News* and most current affairs programmes in the UK. In 1990, he was a guest on BBC TV's *Wogan* chat show. He has written for *The Times*, *Guardian*, *Independent*, *Sun*, *Mirror*, *Spectator*, *New Statesman* and *Tribune*.

He is a member of the National Union of Journalists (NUJ) and Chartered Institute for Public Relations (CIPR), as well as the Royal Television Society (RTS).

Paul is married to Sarah, and they have two sons, Oliver and Alexander.

Acknowledgements

S O MANY PEOPLE have provided advice, assistance and support along the way, it would be invidious to single people out. Many preferred to remain in the shadows. You all know who you are, and I'm very grateful.

I'd like to thank everyone at Biteback, including Iain Dale, Olivia Beattie, Vicky Gilder, Sam Jones and Laurie De Decker.

A very special word of thanks must go to the talented Caitlin Plunkett-Reilly, who provided first-rate research and drafting skills for this book.

Finally, thank you to Sarah, Alexander and Oliver for all their love and support.

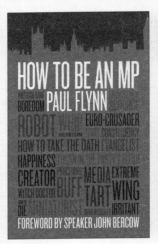
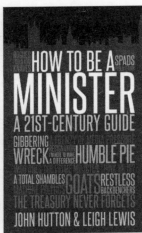
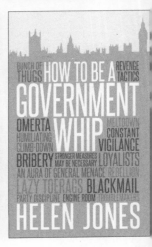

HOW TO BE...

HOW TO BE AN MP

From how to address the crowd, weather marital troubles and socialise at party conference to the all-important Backbenchers' Commandments, *How to Be an MP* is indispensable reading for anyone wishing to make a mark from the back bench and influence proceedings in the House.

HOW TO BE A MINISTER

A fail-safe guide to how to survive as a Secretary of State in Her Majesty's Government, from dealing with civil servants, Cabinet colleagues, the opposition and the media, to coping with the bad times whilst managing the good (and how to resign with a modicum of dignity intact when it all inevitably falls apart).

HOW TO BE A GOVERNMENT WHIP

One of the most misunderstood and oft-caricatured jobs in British politics, whips are the unseen, unsung heroes of the parliamentary system. From the mind-numbing tedium of debates to the dark arts of dealing with rebellious or disaffected members of their 'flock', former whip Helen Jones reveals how they really get business done.